"Calvin's robust defense of (is an excellent reminder of what was a vital concern for the French Reformer and also of his desire to be rigorously biblical and, as such, God-glorifying. Here is a pattern of theological reflection and method truly worthy of emulation."

—MICHAEL A. G. HAYKIN, Professor of Church History, Southern Baptist Theological Seminary

"Calvin's treatise on the secret providence of God shows the Reformer at his theological best and polemically most acute. Like Luther before him, he demonstrates why the doctrine of divine sovereignty lies at the very heart of the Reformation, and why the doctrine is of such singular doctrinal, pastoral, and ecclesiastical importance. It is to be hoped that this new edition will introduce a new generation to Calvin's thinking on this vital matter."

—CARL R. TRUEMAN, Academic Dean and Vice President, Westminster Theological Seminary.

Calumniæ nebu-
LONIS CVIVSDAM, QVI-
bus odio & inuidia grauare conatus est doctrinam Ioh . Caluini de
occulta Dei prouidentia.

IOHANNIS CALVINI AD
easdem responsio.

VVLTVS TVI

PRELVM

IN SVDORE · ASCENSIANVM · VESCERIS PANE.

M. D. LVIII.

Ex officina Conradi Badii.

*Jacob Botillierÿ anno ab homine redempto
1560*

THE SECRET PROVIDENCE OF GOD

JOHN CALVIN

EDITED BY

PAUL HELM

TRANSLATED BY

KEITH GOAD

WHEATON, ILLINOIS

Library of Congress Cataloging-in-Publication Data
Calvin, Jean, 1509–1564
    [Calumniae nebulonis cuiusdam, quibus odio et invidia gravare
conatus est doctrinam Ioh. English]
    The secret providence of God / John Calvin ; edited by Paul
helm ; translated by Keith Goad.—[New ed.].
      p. cm.
    ISBN 978-1-4335-0705-2 (tpb)
    1. Providence and government of God—Christianity. I. Helm, Paul.
II. Goad, Keith. III. Title
BT135.C2713   2010
231'.5—dc22   2009024553

VP		19	18	17	16	15	14	13	12	11	10
13	12	11	10	9	8	7	6	5	4	3	2	1

To the Memory
of
David F. Wright

CONTENTS

PREFACE

John Calvin's *Concerning the Secret Providence of God* has the original title *Calumniae nebulonis cuiusdam, quibus odio et invidia gravare conatus est doctrinam Ioh. Calvini de occulta Dei providentia. Joannis Calvini ad easdem responsio.* It was published by Conrad Badius in 1558. The Latin text is found in *Calvini Opera*.[1]

While we have collaborated closely throughout this project, Keith Goad is chiefly responsible for the translation and Paul Helm for the footnoting and the introduction. We have tried to produce a translation that adheres fairly literally to the original. In order to help the reader, the fourteen articles have been reproduced both in the calumniator's commentary and in Calvin's response. Some of the original long paragraphs have been broken up for easier reading.

Where Calvin provides a reference in the text, we have kept it there. All footnotes are our own. For Calvin's quotations from Scripture we have generally used the ESV. Besides providing direct quotations from Scripture, Calvin sometimes alludes to biblical passages, and where possible the references and sometimes the texts have been supplied in the footnotes. References have also been given for Calvin's various classical allusions. His references to Augustine, the only Christian author that Calvin cites, have also been given in the footnotes in those instances where they have not been provided by Calvin himself. Occasionally, translations of Augustine have

---

[1] vol. 9, pp. 273–318.

also been given in the footnotes, using various translations. The authority for the references to Augustine (where Calvin himself does not provide these) is the monumental work of L. Smits, *Saint Augustin dans l'oeuvre de Jean Calvin* (2 vols.; Assen: van Gorcum, 1956–1957 and 1958). Smits often offers multiple sources for some allusions that Calvin makes to Augustine, but we have supplied one reference or two at the most. The full list of references or possible references can be consulted in Smits (vol. 2, 113–14).

This new edition of Calvin's *Concerning the Secret Providence of God* could not have been prepared without help from others. Among these we particularly wish to thank Martin Cameron, Daniel Hill, Tony Lane, and Grace Mullen. Thanks as well to the Libraries of the Highland Theological College, Dingwall; the Southern Baptist Seminary, Louisville; and the Westminster Theological Seminary, Philadelphia, for various kinds of assistance.

—Keith Goad and Paul Helm

EDITOR'S INTRODUCTION

Concerning the Secret Providence of God (1558) was Calvin's third response to writings that he took to be those of a fellow Frenchman, Sebastian Castellio (1515–1563). Calvin prefaces this defense of his view of God's providence by providing the Castellio material, which is in the form of fourteen articles, ostensibly drawn from Calvin's writings, together with commentaries on each.

The two antagonists had a rather mixed relationship. Castellio met Calvin during the Reformer's time in Strasbourg, and he stayed with Calvin there for a time in 1540. Initially, Calvin seems to have formed a warm attachment to him. He was impressed by his facility with languages, and during 1543–1544, on Calvin's return to Geneva, Castellio was initially employed as rector of the College of Geneva.[1] While in the process of seeking to become a minister he began to fall afoul of the authorities, among other things condemning the Song of Solomon as a lewd book and calling for its removal from the Canon. He also asked Calvin to be a "consultant" for his French translation of the Bible. Somewhat reluctantly Calvin agreed to help him. This led to quarrels over Castellio's general approach to translating Holy Scripture as well as to wrangles over *les mots justes,* and the result was a developing mutual antipathy. Castellio resigned from the college in 1544 and later that year unsuccessfully sought work in Lausanne,

---

[1] I have taken many of the details of Castellio's life, and also bibliographical information, from Hans R. Guggisberg, *Sebastian Castellio 1515–1563, Humanist and Defender of Religious Toleration in a Confessional Age,* trans. and ed. Bruce Gordon (Aldershot: Ashgate 2003).

taking with him a recommendation written by Calvin on behalf of the Genevan clergy. After returning to Geneva, he publicly rebuked the clergy for various alleged failings, and, as a result, he was forced to leave the city permanently. He resided in Basle, working for a time as a proofreader. There in 1551 he published his Latin Bible, dedicated to Edward VI of England, and in 1555 the French Bible (the one begun in Geneva), dedicated to Henry II of France. He was made professor of Greek at the University of Basle in 1553.

Following the execution of Michael Servetus in 1553 Castellio mounted a personal campaign against the Genevan authorities, writing *De haereticis an sint persequendi* in 1554 (under the pseudonym Martinus Bellius), which attacked the then-normal policy of persecuting heretics.[2] Theodore Beza replied to this treatise with *De haereticis a civili magistratu* (1554), which Castellio answered the following year with *De haereticis non puniendis*, this time using the pen-name Basilius Montfort. His attack on persecution has earned for him a reputation as an early modern defender of religious toleration. Castellio also replied to Calvin's work against Servetus, *Defensio orthodoxae fidei de sacra Trinitate*, in his *Contra libellum Calvini in quo ostendere conatur haereticos jure gladii coercendos esse* (1554). He published various other writings, including annotations on the ninth chapter of Romans, of an anti-Augustinian and anti-Reformed flavor. According to Beza, in these annotations Castellio recognized "no decrees of God except concerning things that are good by nature, forging in God a permission contrary to his will, and falsely charging that we make God the author of sin."[3]

---

[2]This was translated into English by Roland Bainton as *Concerning Heretics, Whether They Are to Be Persecuted* (New York: Columbia University Press, 1935).
[3]Bernard Cottret, *Calvin, A Biography*, trans. M. Wallace McDonald (Edinburgh, T & T Clark, 2000), 228.

About the same time, there began what became a series of exchanges with Calvin on predestination and providence, perhaps provoked not only by what Calvin had stated in his *Institutes*, but also by the publication in 1552 of his *Concerning the Eternal Predestination of God*, written against Albertus Pighius and others. Due to the loss of original manuscripts or books, the exact history of the Calvin-Castellio exchanges is rather murky. It appears that Castellio began publicly objecting to Calvin's views of providence and predestination by anonymously circulating (in French) a set of unpublished remarks, now lost.[4] Calvin's first published (or at least circulated) reply to Castellio's objections, amounting to less than five thousand words, was entitled *Responses à certaines calumnies et blasphèmes, dont quelsques malins s'efforcent de rendre la doctrine de la prédestination de Dieu odieuse*. According to Willem de Greef this is also lost,[5] but a Latin translation survives and was published, or republished, as an appendix to *Treze sermons traitons de l'élection gratuite de Dieu en Jacob, et de la rejection en Esau* in 1562.[6] Calvin's reply contains an explicit though rather guarded reference to Castellio; he refers to a "writing which was scattered about," suggesting private circulation rather than publication, and he also mentions certain of its "Articles" and the fact that its author makes a reference to Melanchthon.

---

[4]Later on Castellio, in his semi-autobiographical work *Harpago* (1558), which circulated in manuscript before being posthumously published in 1578, was to deny that some of these writings were, in fact, his. See Guggisberg, *Sebastian Castellio*, 145. But this Introduction is written with the assumption that the generally held belief, shared by Calvin, that Castellio is the author is correct.

[5]Willem de Greef, *The Writings of John Calvin: An Introductory Guide*, trans. Lyle D. Bierma (Grand Rapids, Baker, 1993), 178.

[6]It is this version that was translated into English in 1579 by John Field as *An Answer to certain slanders and blasphemies, wherewith certain evil disposed persons have gone about to bring the doctrine of God's everlasting Predestination into hatred*, and included in Field's translation of Calvin's sermons on Jacob and Esau. A modernized English version of these, together with the piece on predestination, has been published as *Sermons on Election and Reprobation*, foreword by David C. Engelema (Audubon, NJ: Old Paths Publications, 1996).

Castellio's French work, the one now apparently lost, was then followed by a work in Latin, which he arranged to have privately printed in Paris and clandestinely circulated in the Reformed community, including, of course, Geneva. Perhaps there were various products of Castellio's in circulation around this time. In a letter written to the church of Poitiers in February 1555, Calvin himself refers to "papers and books" of Castellio's written against predestination and to Castellio's bad habit of drawing attention to his own virtue and to the viciousness of those who adhered to the doctrine of grace.[7] This Latin work also appears to be lost. Calvin replied to it in 1557 with *Brevis responsio ad diluendas nebulonis cuiusdam calumnias quibus doctrinam de aaeterna Dei praedestinatione foedare conatus est.*[8]

In September 1557, during a visit to Basle, Beza was shown a manuscript of fourteen articles or "calumnies" on providence and predestination, together with a critical commentary, which was due to be published in Paris.[9] The document took the form of an open letter to Calvin. Basle was at this period antipathetic to Calvin's Geneva on a number of issues. Calvin received a manuscript of the work in November and initially hesitated over whether he should offer a reply, but then in January of 1558 he published *Calumiae nebulonis cuiusdam quibus odio et invidia gravare conatus est doctrinam*

---

[7]*Selected Writings of John Calvin*, ed. Henry Beveridge and Jules Bonnet (Grand Rapids: Baker, 1983), 6:143. There is some internal evidence for this in that in *The Secret Providence* Calvin refers to Castellio's comparison of himself to Socrates, to which there is, in fact, no reference in the Fourteen Articles or the commentary. Perhaps this comparison occurs in other papers of Castellio's that Calvin had also seen.

[8]This was translated by Henry Cole as part of his *Calvin's Calvinism* (1855; repr., London: Sovereign Grace Union, 1927; Grand Rapids: Eerdmans, 1940) and there is a modern translation by J. K. S. Reid included in *Calvin: Theological Treatises*, Library of Christian Classics, vol. 20 (London: SCM Press, 1964). Henry Cole (1792–1852), educated at Clare Hall, Cambridge, was an Anglican clergyman with high Calvinist views and a taste for controversy. He took up various contemporary causes such as opposition to the uniformitarian geology of Adam Sidgwick and to the teaching of Edward Irving. Cole also translated Luther's *Bondage of the Will*.

[9]Guggisberg, *Sebastian Castellio*, 139f.

Ioh. Calvini de occulta Dei providential: Johannis Calvini ad easdem responsio.[10] There are some signs of hasty preparation. As the title of Calvin's response indicates, Castellio's calumnies are reproduced together with Calvin's replies. While Calvin does not mention Castellio by name, there are internal details which reveal clearly that he is confident that Castellio is the author.

As noted, the work is in the form of fourteen articles claiming to set out Calvin's views, with a commentary on each article. The anonymous author wrote as if he were a third party, communicating the articles (as if prepared by others) and the accompanying commentary to Calvin in a "letter," and inviting his response. It is this response of Calvin's, prefaced by the fourteen articles and Castellio's commentary on them, that is now freshly translated into English.

There have been two earlier English translations. In 1840 James Lillie published *Calvin on Secret Providence* (New York: Robert Carter), but this has, in general, been little noticed.[11] In the middle years of the nineteenth century Henry Cole translated three closely related works of Calvin's: *Concerning the Eternal Predestination of God* written against Albert Pighius and others; *A Brief Reply* against Castellio; and *A Defence of the Secret Providence of God*, publishing them together as *Calvin's Calvinism*. However, in his treatment of the first and third of these pieces, Cole silently rearranged Calvin's mate-

---

[10]*Calvini Opera*, 9:257–318. For full bibliographical details of the work see *Bibliotheca Calviniana*, Rodolpe Peter and Jean-Francois Gilmont (Geneva: Librairie Droz, 1991–2000) 2:663–68. Theodore Beza also published a reply to Castellio, *Ad Seb. Castellionis Calumnias, quibus unicum salutis nostrae fundamentum, i.e. aeternam Dei praedestinationem evertere nititur, responsio* (Geneva, 1558; 2nd ed., Geneva, 1582).
[11]This has been reprinted (2008) by Kessinger (Whitefish, MT). James Lillie (1800–1875) was a Scottish Presbyterian minister who emigrated to the U.S. in 1833, ministering in various churches. He translated Calvin's work while at Rhinebeck, New York. He returned for a time to Scotland before going back to the U.S. For a time he was professor of chemistry at the University of Iowa but negotiated an exchange with the professor of classical languages! He also published *Bishops and Councils*, 1870.

rial. The last section of *Concerning the Eternal Predestination of God* was dropped from his translation of that work, and instead it became the opening section of *A Defence of the Secret Providence of God*. So Calvin's *Defence* is measurably shorter than the reader of Cole's translation of the book of that name would appreciate, just as his translation of *Concerning the Eternal Predestination of God* lacks the last section.

The present translation of the work is of the Latin text with no additions or subtractions, and it attempts to avoid the florid paraphrasing and severe and rather excitable tone of Cole's translation; though given the antagonists' own language, harshness and rudeness cannot always be avoided.

The work provides us with a small window onto the boisterous, argumentative years of the Reformation, not in this case to the main conflicts but to the skirmishes initiated by some of its lesser characters, such as Pighius and Servetus and, of course, Castellio. One is also immediately reminded that this was a somewhat different world from ours, one of sharply edged though often subtle theological doctrines, frequently communicated equally sharply and also crudely.[12] This was a time in which there was little opportunity for the exercise of toleration; it was the age of the Inquisition, of the rack and the thumbscrew and of the persecution and execution of "heretics" by whoever had political power.

In this exchange between Castellio and Calvin one is also made aware not only of those who, children of their time (late medievalism), stood by the letter of Scripture, but also of the beginnings of a more liberal and superficially more

---

[12]Among those who were otherwise sympathetic to Calvin's outlook, on the publication of the work Wolfgang Musculus wrote to him complaining about the harshness of his language, while Peter Marty Vermigli, who also wrote to Calvin, was unqualified in his praise (see the *Bibliotheca Calviniana* for details). However, Guggisberg's claims that the response was "venomous" and "without restraint" and that it expressed Calvin's "intestinal hatred" of his one-time supporter (144–45) are considerable exaggerations.

appealing Christianity, of a mentality willing and able to pick and choose between what was regarded as the spirit and the letter of Scripture and also impatient with doctrinal nuance. Castellio was perceptive in recognizing, in the closing section of his attack, that between the theological outlook that he was representing and Calvin's views there is a conflict between two contrary conceptions of God. One is benign and universalistic in his intent but ultimately ineffectual, whereas the other is resolute in grace as well as in judgment, always in control, with ends that he unfailingly brings to pass.

Calvin's inflexible, predictable, rhetorical strategy and Castellio's rather knockabout caricaturing of the central features, as well as the nuances of Calvin's views, reflect this division. Calvin was gentle and accommodating to those whom he reckoned were on his side, who were sympathetic to his doctrine and to the work of reform, or who at least did not oppose him. But he is pitiless and unflattering towards those such as Castellio who openly crossed him. By contrast, Castellio was not in the least defensive, for he was out to create a different religious and theological impression, to set a different tone, not so much to play Calvin at his own game as to ridicule and intentionally misrepresent his views in the name of the common man. In the comments on the fourteen articles, he presents himself in the guise of a worried, would-be supporter of Calvin. He references Calvin's opponents as if he is mediating or attempting to mediate between the two outlooks, but he clearly emerges as Calvin's opponent. To Calvin's intense irritation, here is a man, once a friend and follower, who is now impatient of the carefully crafted subtleties that Calvin sometimes uses to advance his position, and above all contemptuous of the God whose interests Calvin sought to advance. Even their Protestantism provides them with little common ground.

There are other personal touches in the text worth noting; for example, Calvin refers several times to his writings and his reputation. In 1558 he was at the height of his powers and his personal authority in Geneva and beyond. Calvin recognized his influence and was extremely self-conscious of the considerable corpus of his published works and their wide circulation and influence. He saw himself through these writings as having adopted a very public position of leadership in the Reform movement. This prominence clearly gave him, he thought, the not unreasonable expectation that those who aimed to refute his views should, by quoting them accurately, provide at least some evidence that they had read him carefully. He was upset by what he regarded as the slapdash and inaccurate summaries and quotations from his writings.

Although the work was anonymous and he does not mention Castellio by name, Calvin refers to his earlier friendship and also makes a rather oblique reference to Castellio's alleged theft of some firewood.[13] Castellio was clearly a person capable of a more scholarly and deferential approach than he offers in the fourteen articles, and one is left with the thought that part of his strategy may have been to treat Calvin offhandedly in public, and even, by the crude way in which he writes, to bait Calvin, provoking him into some theological indiscretion. If so, he must have been disappointed by Calvin's replies; it is evident that he continued resolutely to maintain the doctrinal position on providence and predestination laid out in the editions of the *Institutes* from 1539 onward as well as in

---

[13]Calvin may have got hold of the wrong end of the stick, so to speak; for later on (in his *Harpago*) Castellio protested that he did not steal the wood but was merely taking driftwood in order to heat his house.

his *Concerning the Eternal Predestination of God*, published, as we have noted, about five years earlier than *The Secret Providence of God*.

In these works he presents providence and predestination together, physically together in the case of both works, though, as is well known, in the 1559 *Institutes* he was to separate the treatment of providence from that of predestination. However, the two ideas were closely connected in his thought. Such providence/predestination was "absolute"; that is, it was not conditioned by any human merit or by God's foreknowledge of any other such preconditions, nor is providence to be regarded as a mere general superintendence of the creation. Rather it reaches down to every detail, including the intricacies of human action. Thus Calvin's belief about predestination/providence also embraced the fall and the propagation of original sin, as well as that those predestined to life according to God's foreknowledge and election were only a minority of the human race and the predestination of the elect had its counterpart in the perdition of the reprobate.

Calvin's response to Castellio's comments is of theological and (to a lesser extent) philosophical interest for two or three distinct reasons. In the first place, it underlines Calvin's willingness, in defending his ideas, to adopt a *disputatio* method, if not always a *disputatio* style of a formal kind. As Richard Muller has noted, although the *Institutes*, for example, is not scholastic either in method or tone, nevertheless Calvin regarded it as an exposition of the main articles of the faith, and as such it contains a number of "dogmatic disputations."[14] *The Secret Providence* has more of the overt form of a printed *disputatio* than the *Institutes*. Of course, it

---

[14]*The Unaccommodated Calvin* (New York: Oxford University Press, 2000), 105.

is true that a "reply" to Castellio's work would not have been very intelligible without the fourteen articles and their commentary side by side. Nevertheless, in printing them, followed by his responses, Calvin adopts what is close to the style of a formal *disputatio*. It is natural to think of the articles as fourteen theses, the associated commentary as the arguments supporting these, and Calvin's replies as his formal responses. Calvin's language, despite the personal contempt for Castellio that he expresses, particularly his talk of "arguments," his desire to avoid self-contradiction, his use of the dilemma, and his reference to Castellio's logical errors, all point to a willingness to use a formalized style when the occasion called for it.

In the Bolsec controversy (1551–1552) Calvin had already faced similar objections over his understanding of predestination to those that Castellio raised. Jerome Bolsec was a former Carmelite friar, later turned physician/theologian, who in Geneva openly denounced Calvin's understanding of reprobation.[15] Bolsec's chief claim appears to have been that "in the order of time unbelief precedes the decree to reprobate."[16] This raised issues about whether election is upon foreseen faith, on God's authorship of evil, and the two wills in God,[17] and debates were held regarding the very same texts, such as 1 Timothy 2:4 and Ezekiel 33:11, as Castellio was later to cite. Although Calvin wanted the matter dropped, Bolsec was imprisoned, tried, and expelled from the city. After his expulsion he had connections with Berne but did not settle there. He returned to Roman Catholicism and died in Lyons in 1585. Calvin did not write directly against Bolsec (except

---

[15] An account of the Bolsec affair may be found in *The Register of the Company of Pastors of Geneva in the Time of Calvin*, ed. and trans. Philip E. Hughes (Grand Rapids, MI: Eerdmans, 1966), 137–81.

[16] Hughes, *The Register*, 143.

[17] Ibid., 164.

as part of the court proceedings), but the conflict blew up during the time that he was writing his *Concerning the Eternal Predestination of God* against Pighius and Georgius and may have influenced what he wrote.

The fourteen articles have three or four interrelated and repeated themes. To begin with, there are two conceptual issues, which have to do respectively with the senses of divine providence and divine foreknowledge. The first arises because, in Calvin's judgment, Castellio flattens his distinctions between secret, particular providence and a general superintendence, and the second because of Castellio's subordination of divine providence to a weaker sense of divine foreknowledge than Calvin's. Castellio blurs the first distinction by promoting the idea that God's providence has a discretionary character that allows people to choose between alternatives, the choice being in no sense willed by God but merely generally permitted by him and foreknown by him. He pays no respect to Calvin's distinction between "bare" and "willing" permission, so he misrepresents and even misquotes Calvin, much to the Reformer's annoyance. Similarly with divine foreknowledge. For Castellio this idea does not possess the causal and volitional connotations of Calvin's own understanding, but divine foreknowledge is simply God's awareness of what is to come to pass as a result of human choices, not what he has decreed to come to pass.

Castellio's general line is that the distinction between God's willing permission and God's decree is merely nominal, so that, in effect, if by his decree God wills all that comes to pass then he wills evil in precisely the same fashion as he wills good, and he is responsible for evil in precisely the same sense that he is responsible for good. This not only compromises God's character but also calls into question another of Calvin's nuances: his distinction between "two wills" in God—"will" in the sense of what God decrees and "will" in the sense of what God commands. Castellio's preference for understanding divine providence as "bare" providence and divine foreknowledge as "mere" foreknowledge and his rejection of the stronger senses of these terms lead him to ridicule what in fact are Calvin's central and controlling distinctions in this debate.

Castellio argues that if, as Calvin claims, God controls whatever comes to pass, then how can he sincerely command what is at odds with what he decrees shall comes to pass? Surely, if God wills an action, say, an evil action, then he wants that action to occur, and if so, then how can he sincerely forbid it and how can that action be evil? Castellio has some fun at Calvin's expense in claiming that Calvin's doctrine obliterates moral distinctions, making it difficult to distinguish between God and the Devil! (Article 3). So he represents Calvin's views as "all the crimes that have been accomplished by any man are the good and just works of God" (Article 4) and "the will of God is the supreme cause of the hardness of men's hearts" (Article 9).

Castellio's fire is directed at Calvin's inability to *demonstrate* how what is not commanded by God can also be willed by God in a significant sense, and this opens up what for Calvin turns out to be the central issue. This is Castellio's fondness for preferring his own reason to what for Calvin is the clear teaching of the Word of God about the Lord's decreeing evil and his use of that evil to further his own purposes. Castellio believes that by reason, common sense, and the use of certain apt analogies, he can clear up or rather avoid what Calvin regards as divine mysteries, the fact that these matters are beyond our full understanding, being "ineffable." Calvin freely recognizes that we cannot altogether see how what God commands and what he decrees are part of his one simple will, and we cannot presently fathom the reasons that God has for electing some and bypassing others. Nevertheless, for Calvin it is sufficient that Scripture repeatedly affirms such things (along with claiming that God is not himself sinful, not "the author of sin"). We cannot fully comprehend how it is that these things—God's universal, absolute decree and man's culpability for evil—can be consistent, not even with the help of the distinction between primary and secondary causation, or of the doctrine of the two wills, or of God's willing permission.

Both providence, God's government of his entire creation, and predestination, the destining of some—those elected to grace and salvation to eternal life through Jesus Christ—are the work of God's decree. But what of those not elected, the reprobates? It is this issue and the doctrine of original sin that, according to Calvin, it presupposes is one of the flashpoints of the exchange. A central part of Calvin's account of reprobation lies in his doctrine of God's two wills, between the *secret* and the *revealed* will of God. It should be noted that neither this distinction nor the other nuances that we have noted, are Calvin's invention. The doctrine of the two wills is standard medieval fare, codified as the distinction between the will of God's good pleasure and the will of his sign. And the distinction between a general permission and a willing permission goes back at least as far as Augustine, as Calvin shows. Yet perhaps it is true that Calvin's denial of "bare" foreknowledge takes him beyond standard medievalism.

God's revealed law establishes moral standards and obligations which, as is known from experience, are widely flouted, for men and women frequently act immorally. But given God's providential government of his creation and also his predestination of the saints, such immoralities are also willed by God, for they are a part of his "particular" providence, the character of which is equitable and just. To use two examples cited by Calvin, God prohibits incest, and yet he willed that Absalom should commit incest. He forbids deceit and yet willed that Jesus should be betrayed, and so on. What is hidden from us, the factor that leads to Calvin's habitual reference to "secret" providence, are God's purposes or reasons for willingly permitting the particular occasions of evil that occur and for denying salvation to many.

Calvin notes that in phrases such as "God's secret will" and "God's revealed will" the word *will* is used equivocally. These are not only two different senses of *will*, but insofar as the revealed law is flouted, God's will in this sense is at odds with his divine decree. But Calvin hardly helps his own cause when he occasionally uses expressions such as "God wills what he does not will." For if God wills what he does not will, there is a contradiction at the very heart of what, according to Calvin, God wills. But he vehemently denies this, so the two divine wills need to be carefully distinguished.

Then there is the problem of divine permission. On this, the reader of *The Secret Providence of God* may initially be as puzzled as Castellio said that he was, for Calvin both affirms and denies that God permits evil. How can this be? Following Augustine, in his *Enchiridion* and elsewhere, Calvin denies that God merely permits evil but affirms that he willingly permits it. That is, God's permission is *particular*; it concerns every particular evil occurrence and is not a general superintendence of events, so it is *willing* permission and not *mere* permission. Does God permit evil or not? Answer: yes and no. No, he does not merely permit evil, but yes, he willingly permits this particular evil and that particular evil—all evils. But how can God willingly permit what he forbids, and how can he willingly permit what is evil without himself being tainted by the evil? Castellio's view is that the only way of coping with these questions is to abandon both the ideas of willing permission, that of two wills and that of divine foreknowledge as a causal power, and instead to trust common sense.

One has the impression, from *The Secret Providence of God* and from other writings such as the *Institutes*, that deploying this distinction is not Calvin's preferred option just because of the confusion between "willing permission" and "bare permission" that it engenders. But it is going too far to say that Calvin repudiates the idea of the divine permission of evil. Nevertheless, he seems to think that as soon as people hear the word *permission* in connection with evil, they immediately conclude that this is bare or general permission, as when a child is permitted by her teacher either to swim or to run. In granting such permission the teacher gives the power of discretion to the child but is not *in* the decision (whichever it is) in the sense in which, according to Calvin, God is in the occurrence of every evil in virtue of his decreeing it. Bare permission fits snugly in the theological thinking of someone whose God is not all-decreeing.

Whether or not Calvin did have this distaste for the language of permission, he provides an underpinning for it in what he says about the distinction between divine and human intentions. God decrees evil by a wise and all good intention that is hierarchically higher than the evil intention of the creature's. Furthermore, God not only decrees the election and predestination of his saints but positively effects this by the illuminating and regenerating powers of his Spirit. So Calvin does not qualify or apologize for scriptural assertions about God's decreeing of evil or even of his commanding evil, because what God decrees is an evil intention that is not his own intention, for his intention in decreeing evil is not itself evil. At the same time, he is able to argue that Castellio's view of God's relation to good, particularly to the redemption of men and women through Jesus Christ, is ultimately ineffectual, since Castellio reduces God's will to the bare foreknowledge of what people freely choose.

We have noted the doctrinal and metaphysical differences between the two antagonists, but behind these are important epistemological distinctions. In Calvin's eyes Castellio's epistemological approach to Scripture, with its emphasis upon common sense, has two important and rather ominous defects. First, Castellio is fond of employing analogies that he devises and then applies to Scripture. These provide him with an interpretative lens. For example, he uses the analogy between God as our Father and fathers in both human society and the animal kingdom. Such fathers care for their children equitably and equally, and can our heavenly Father be different? How can the one heavenly Father have children he elects and those he passes by? For Calvin, God has the right to discriminate and choose, even though his reasons for choosing are inscrutable to us. He is our Father in the sense that he is our creator and sustainer, but he has the rights of a creator, and this must never be forgotten. Castellio's fondness for analogies that fly in the face of what Calvin regards as the clear teaching of Scripture touches on what he sees as Castellio's second epistemological deficiency: his intolerance of and impatience over any attribution of mystery or unaccountability to God's ways. Calvin is ready to emphasize human limitations in understanding or explaining God's ways. Castellio is not.

These differences are symptomatic of two different conceptions of God, as Castellio notes in his closing remarks. Calvin certainly does not demur, though quite understandably he objects to the personally insulting way in which Castellio writes about him and his followers. In his theology Calvin never resorts to paradox or logical incoherence to address theological problems, even though he readily recognizes God's inaccessibility. But how can his account of God possibly be consistent? How can he have two wills and not generally permit evil but willingly permit this evil and that evil? How can he proclaim the freeness of his grace and at the same time elect and predestinate only a small minority of the human race to salvation? Calvin's response to such questions is threefold: to affirm the meaning and truth of the scriptural data that call forth these distinctions, to resolutely refuse to apply analogies to God that are not themselves warranted by Scripture, and to affirm (also on scriptural precedent) that God's ways are mysterious and unfathomable. Castellio's strategy is to ignore Calvin's nuances and to straightforwardly charge Calvin's God with being the author of evil. Dialectically, Calvin is at something of a disadvantage at such points because he has to answer the charge that God is the author of sin by deploying his distinctions, as well as by appealing to divine inscrutability, and this procedure is made to seem contrived and self-serving to someone as impatient as Castellio.

It is not clear that this exchange changed anyone's mind—certainly not Calvin's. What of Castellio? He died about six years after the circulation of his *Calumnies*, in 1563, but not before writing a good deal more on these topics. His direct reply to *The Secret Providence of God* was *Harpago, sive Defensio ad authorem libri, cui titulus est, Calumniae nebulonis.* This was finished in May 1558 but only published posthumously.[18] *Harpago* means "harpoon" or "grappling hook" and is probably intended as a reference to his response to Calvin's charge that he stole wood. The book was republished in Gouda in 1613 and so was able to contribute to the rise of the Remonstrants in the Reformed church in Holland.[19]

It is of course difficult to extrapolate beyond the lives of Calvin and Castellio, but it may be that what Calvin writes against Castellio in 1558 provides us with some clues as to how he would have responded to Jacobus Arminius or, if not how he would have responded, how someone who continued to hold the views expressed in *The Secret Providence of God* would have responded. We can at least say this much: Castellio's concepts of divine foreknowledge and the relation of the will of God to evil, his rejection of the two-wills doctrine and the idea of willing permission, are also characteristic of and central to the theology of Jacobus Arminius. For Arminius, as for Castellio, divine foreknowledge is conditional divine knowledge of future actions, and the divine permission of sin

---

[18]It was published as part of a set, "Dialogues": *Dialogue IIII De praedestinatione, De electione, De libero arbitrio, De fide. Eiusdem opuscula quaedam lectu dignissima quorum inscriptions versa pagella ostendet Omnia nunc primum in lucem data* (Aresdorffij: per Theophil. Philadeiph. [= Basel: P. Pernal], 1578). Reliqua, quae hoc libellum coninentur haec sunt: I *Quaestio, An perfecta legi Dei ab homine per Spiritum Sanctum obediri posit* (1562); 2. *Responsio ad D. Mart Borrhaum, De praedestinatione* (1562); *Defensio adversus libellum cuius titulus est, Calumniae Nebulonis* (1558); 4. *De Calumnia liber anus* (1557). "Harpago" was dropped from the published version of the title.

[19]Guggisberg, *Sebastian Castellio*, 242f.

is a bare rather than a willing permission, though expressed in a rather more developed and polished way than the rather crude or inchoate theological style of Castellio. One might go so far as to appropriate Richard Muller's description of Arminius's thinking as a "theology of creation" (rather than as a "theology of grace") to Castellio's attack on Calvin via his commentary on the fourteen articles.[20]

---

[20]For an account of these themes in Arminius, see Richard A Muller, *God, Creation and Providence in the Thought of Jacob Arminius* (Grand Rapids, Baker, 1993), especially chaps. 9 and 12. The remarks about Arminius's theology of creation appear on p. 268.

THE

SECRET PROVIDENCE

OF GOD

CALUMNIATOR'S PREFACE TO
CERTAIN ARTICLES

Your doctrine certainly has many supporters, John Calvin, a man who nearly all men renown but who likewise has many adversaries. I truly desire there to be one doctrine, just as there is one truth, and for all to agree in the same way. If it is possible, I believe you should be warned, in a friendly manner, what is being said against your doctrine, so that you might refute it if it is false and then might send us your refutation. We could then stand together against the adversaries; and you might produce another argument of this kind that might be understood by the general public.

There are, moreover, many who dissent from you in many things. However, at present I will put the others to one side for another time. I will present the case of the one argument concerning fate or predestination, since this great knot is causing a disturbance in the church that we desire to be removed. The arguments of your adversaries are strong, and it is not possible to refute them from the books that you have thus far published.

However, certain articles concerning this argument have been extracted from your books and are being circulated. I will put these in no particular order. In the next place I will present your adversaries' position as they are accustomed to set it forth so that you might see what response is called for.

Articles on Predestination
Extracted from John Calvin's
Latin and French Writings

1) By his bare and pure will God creates the greater part of the world for destruction.

2) God not only predestined Adam to damnation but also predestined the causes of his damnation, whose fall he not only foresaw, but by his secret and eternal decree he ordained that he would perish. In order that this would come about in due time, God provided the apple for the purpose of the fall.

3) The sins that are committed are not solely by God's permission but are committed even by the very will of God. For as far as sin is concerned, it is frivolous to make a distinction between the permission and the will of God. Whoever makes this distinction wishes to please God by flattery and adulation.

4) All the crimes that have been accomplished by any man are the good and just works of God.

5) No adultery, theft, or murder is committed without the will of God being involved (Inst. 14.44.)[1]

6) Scripture clearly testifies that crimes are planned not only by the will of God but even by his authority.

7) Whatever men bring about when they sin, they do so by the will of God, so much so that the will of God often clashes with his precepts.

8) The hardening of Pharaoh, indeed even his stubbornness of soul and rebellion, was the work of God. Moses testifies to this, according to whom the whole rebellion of Pharaoh is to be attributed to the will of God.

---

[1]This is a reference to the 1539 edition of the *Institutes*.

9) The will of God is the supreme cause of the hardness of men's hearts.

10) Satan is a liar by the command of God.

11) God grants the will to perform evil. Furthermore, he prompts perverse and dishonest affections, not just permissively, but effectually, in order to further his own glory.

12) The impious, in their impiety, produce more of God's work than their own.

13) From the perspective of God we sin necessarily, whether we sin on account of our own purpose or by accident.

14) Whatever perversions men perpetrate by their own will, those also proceed from the will of God.

THESE ARE THE ARTICLES AGAINST WHICH YOU MUST CONSIDER HOW TO STATE YOUR CASE

AGAINST THE FIRST ARTICLE

Article 1: By his bare and pure will God creates the greater part of the world for destruction.

Concerning the First Article, your calumniators declare that it is contrary to both nature and Scripture. With respect to nature, they maintain that every creature naturally loves its own offspring. This nature is given to them by God, and consequently God also loves his own offspring. He would not cause his creatures to love their own offspring if he did not also love his. They prove this by reasoning from Isaiah 66:9 where God said, "Shall I bring to the point of birth and not cause to bring forth?" By this he has said, "What I cause others to do, this I also do. I cause others to give birth, therefore I also give birth." Hence by analogy they argue, "God causes his creatures to love their offspring; therefore, he also loves his own offspring."

All men are the offspring of God, for God is the Father of Adam from whom all men are born. Therefore, God loves all men. But to create simply for the purpose of destruction is not an act of love but an act of hatred. Therefore, he did not create anyone for destruction. Similarly, to create is the work of love, not of hatred. Therefore, God created all men out of love, not out of hatred. In the same way, no beast (much less man) is so cruel that it wills to create its young for misery. How much less is this true of God! Could we suppose that he is inferior to the wolf? Christ argues in this way: "If you then, who are evil, know how to give good gifts to your children, how much more will your Father who is in heaven give good things to those who ask him!" (Matt. 7:11). Your calumniators argue, suppose Calvin is evil, yet even he does not wish to beget a son for misery; how much less would God? They say these and other similar things about nature.

On the other hand, concerning Scripture your calumniators argue as follows. God saw all that he had made to be very good; therefore, the man he made was very good. If we suppose that he created that same man for destruction, he then created what is good for destruction and he loves to destroy what is good. It is blasphemous even to think in such a way. Likewise, God created one man and he placed him in paradise, which is a life of blessing. Therefore, he created all men for a blessed life, for all are created in the one man. And if all men are fallen in Adam, it is necessary that all men stood in Adam and exist in the same condition as Adam. Again, "I have no pleasure in the death of the wicked."[1] Again, "God desires all people to be saved and to come to the knowledge of the truth."[2] Again, if God created the majority of the world for perdition, it follows that his anger is greater than his mercy. However, Scripture declares that he is slow to anger and quick to mercy. It also declares that his anger extends only to the third and fourth generations, but that his mercy will be known even to a thousand generations.

---

[1] Ezek. 33:11.
[2] 1 Tim. 2:4.

AGAINST THE SECOND ARTICLE

Article 2: God not only predestined Adam to damnation but also predestined the causes of his damnation, whose fall he not only foresaw, but by his secret and eternal decree he ordained that he would perish. In order that this would come about in due time, God provided the apple for the purpose of the fall.

Your calumniators say that the second article is the doctrine of the Devil, and they demand of us, Calvin, that we show them where this is written in the Word of God.

AGAINST THE THIRD ARTICLE

Article 3: The sins that are committed are not solely by God's permission but are committed even by the very will of God. For as far as sin is concerned, it is frivolous to make a distinction between the permission and the will of God. Whoever makes this distinction wishes to please God by flattery and adulation.

About the third article, concerning the difference between will and permission, they say: Calvin claims to be a prophet of God, but we say that he is a prophet of the Devil. It is clear that one of us must be speaking falsehood. For if he is a prophet of God, we lie. But if he is a prophet of the Devil, he himself lies when he says that he is a prophet of God. What if both of these are the will of God? That is, if it is the will of God that Calvin is a prophet of God, and God wills also that we say he is a prophet of the Devil, then he wills a contradiction, and this is impossible. For if God wills a lie, he does not will the truth. Also if he wills the truth, he does not will a lie. From which it follows that if God wills that one party speaks the truth, he does not will the other to lie. But one party certainly lies. Therefore, they lie not from the will of God but from the permission of God. Therefore, there is a difference in God between his permission and his will.

There are many clear examples that point to the difference between God's permission and his will. Ezekiel 20:39, where, after God reproved his people with many words because they refused to obey his commandments, says, "Go serve every one of you his idols, now and hereafter, if you will not listen to me." It is as if he said, "I permit you to remain in your lust after you were not willing to obey my commandments." This seems to be the same as what he previously said in the same chapter: "Because they had not obeyed my rules . . . I gave them statutes that were not good" (24–25). The God of Israel did not give commands that were not good, for all of God's commands are good. But since they repudiated the good commands of God, he forsook them, and being forsaken by God, they fell into following evil commandments. Just as being deserted by the father, or rather when his father was forsaken, the prodigal son fell into ruin in his luxury. And just as Paul said, "because they refused to love the truth and so be saved. Therefore God sends them a strong delusion, so that they may believe what is false" (2 Thess. 2:10–11).

This appears to be the same even in Amos 4:4–5: "Come to Bethel and transgress . . . for so you love to do." So it is today. Men who do not wish to obey God, who say that he does not will sin, say God permits spirits of deception to exist, like your own, who teach that God wills sin. He also permits those who do not wish to obey the truth to obey a lie.

Additionally, your calumniators point to a passage in Zechariah (12),[3] where God says that he is angry with the nations who are at rest because when he was lightly angry with Israel, they furthered the evil. That is, they greatly vexed

---

[3]The reference given appears to be a misprint. The likely reference is Zech. 1:15: "And I am exceedingly angry with the nations that are at ease; for while I was angry but a little, they furthered the disaster." In his response Calvin offers comments on this verse.

the Israelites more than the anger of God required. Therefore this was by the permission of God, not by his will.

They also point to a similar example from the prophet Obed, who reproves the Israelites because they greatly afflicted Judah more than the anger of God required (2 Chron. 28:9). These calumniators also point to the example of the prodigal son, which I have already touched on. It would be absurd for you to say that he lived his luxurious life by the will of his father. Therefore this must have been by his permission. In the same way your calumniators say that the guilty are the prodigal children of God. They sin not by the will of God but by his permission. Likewise, Christ asked, "Do you want to go away as well?" (John 6:67). Christ certainly did not bring it about that they departed, but he permitted them to do so.

Finally, they point to the fact that the difference between permission and will is a matter of common sense. When Christ taught divine things he followed common sense. If common sense is taken away, then all the parables of Christ will be nullified, for we interpret these parables by means of common sense.

AGAINST THE FOURTH ARTICLE

Article 4: All the crimes that have been accomplished by any man are the good and just works of God.

Against the fourth article your calumniators exclaim, "Woe to those who call evil good and good evil" (Isa. 5:20). Now, if sin is a good and righteous work of God, it follows that righteousness would be an evil and an unrighteous work of God, for righteousness is entirely contrary to sin. If sin is righteous, it follows that unrighteousness is righteous, for sin is unrighteousness. If sin is a work of God, it follows that God brings about sin; and if he brings sin about, then according to Christ he is a slave to sin. If sin is a work of God, and Christ was offered up in order that sin might be destroyed, then he was offered up in order that the work of God might be destroyed. But if Christ came in order that the work of the Devil might be destroyed (as Peter testified),[4] what then is the work of the Devil? If sin is the righteous work of God, then God hates and punishes his own righteous work. Therefore, it is unrighteous. And if it is presented to them that sin is not sin to God, your calumniators answer, to whom then is it sin? Or for what reason does he hate himself? Or for what reason is sin called sin unless it is contrary to the law—not man's law, but God's? If sin is the work of God, then God brings about sin. And if God brings about sin, he sins, just as if he brings about righteousness, he is righteous.

And if God sins, on what grounds does he reject those who sin? So is it not a better thing for him to decree men to sin, so that they might be imitators of him? A father ought to desire the same thing for his offspring. "Be holy," it is said, "for I am holy" (Lev. 11:44; 1 Pet. 1:16). Therefore, the very same argument will be deployed: "You must perform sin, because I have performed sin."

AGAINST THE FIFTH AND SIXTH ARTICLES

Article 5: No adultery, theft, or murder is committed without the will of God being involved (Inst. 14.44.).

Article 6: Scripture clearly testifies that crimes are planned not only by the will of God but even by his authority.

Against the fifth and sixth arguments the calumniators and many others declare that this consequence is of the greatest

---

[4]This appears to be a slip. The allusion is presumably to 1 John 3:8.

importance: if God wills sin and is the author of sin, then he himself will be punished. For all sin will be judged with respect to the author. If God wills sin, then the Devil does not will sin. That is to say, the idea that the Devil is God is a complete contradiction. If God wills sin, he loves sin; and if he loves sin, he hates righteousness. If God wills sin, he is more wicked than many men, for there are many men who do not wish to sin. In fact, the nearer someone draws to the nature of God, the less he wills to sin. Why else would Paul say, "For I do not do the good I want, but the evil I do not want is what I keep on doing" (Rom. 7:19)? Why does Paul not will what God wills? Or does Paul will what God does not will? Finally, your calumniators ask where Scripture testifies that these evil acts are planned not only by God's will but even by his authority.

AGAINST THE SEVENTH ARTICLE

Article 7: Whatever men bring about when they sin, they do so by the will of God, so much so that the will of God often clashes with his precepts.

The calumniators ask concerning the seventh article: if the will of God often contends with his command, how can it be known when he wills or when he does not will what he commands? If Calvin says what God commands must always be done, whether he wills it or does not will it, it follows that God sometimes wills himself to be resisted. For instance, if God commands me not to commit adultery and yet wills that I commit adultery, and yet I ought not to commit adultery, then I ought to do what is contrary to his will. Now, when he sincerely commands all Israel, "You shall not commit adultery," does he will that all should not commit adultery or that part of the people should commit adultery and another part should not?

Calvin, these calumniators ask for a direct answer to this question. If you say that he wills some to commit adultery and some not to commit adultery, then God himself will be contrary to the commands that he gives. They also say, if he commands one thing and wills another, if he has sweetness in his mouth and bitterness in his heart, then God is a hypocrite. If you respond to these objections by asserting, "God has two contrary wills within himself, one public that is clear in his commands, another hidden," then they ask, "Who revealed this hidden will to Calvin?" For if Calvin and his followers know it, then it is no longer hidden, and if they do not know it, how can they possibly affirm what they are ignorant of?

They also say that it is not possible for two contradictory statements to be the same at the same time and in the same place. However, you advance the fact that to will and not to will are the same, but they are contrary. If God has two wills contrary to one another, it is plausible to suppose that Calvin—one who evidently imitates God—has two wills, the one that he declares, the other that he privately intends to will. Therefore, I refuse to believe a man who is clearly two-tongued, double-hearted, and double-willed.

Also, if God commands righteousness and wills unrighteousness, it follows that the Devil commands unrighteousness and wills righteousness. And if God wills one thing by declaring something else and still does not sin, it follows that if any person imitates him in this, he does not sin, for it is certainly not a vice to be an imitator of God. Therefore, it is lawful for man to be instructed, "Lie! Say one thing and carry on another way in your heart." In this way you may be a liar like your father who says one thing and wills another.

They also ask, according to which will is the Lord speaking when he commands his people to pray "Your will be done" (Matt. 6:10) and "Whoever does the will of my Father in heaven is my brother and sister and mother" (Matt. 12:50)?

Also from Paul, "You call yourself a Jew and rely on the law and boast in God and know his will and approve what is excellent, because you are instructed from the law" (Rom. 2:17). Certainly here is the will of God. That which he commands in the law, if it is good (and it certainly is), must necessarily be contrary to that which is evil. Indeed, whatever is good is contrary to whatever is evil. There is also that well-known saying of Christ's: "How often would I have gathered your children together . . . and you would not!" (Luke 13:34). Certainly Christ speaks of the public will, the one which he revealed in many ways. But if Christ had another will contrary to this one, then his whole life would have been a clear contradiction, and this is too dreadful even to contemplate.

Finally, they say, if God commands one thing and wills another, it is not two wills but deceit, for whoever declares himself to will what he does not will utters a deception. The commands of his Word are not what he wills; rather, it is his will to deceive.

AGAINST THE EIGHTH AND NINTH ARTICLES

Article 8: The hardening of Pharaoh, indeed even his stubbornness of soul and rebellion, was the work of God. Moses testifies to this, according to whom the whole rebellion of Pharaoh is to be attributed to the will of God.

Article 9: The will of God is the supreme cause of the hardness of men's hearts.

Concerning the eighth and ninth articles your calumniators ask, what did Moses mean when he wrote, "Still Pharaoh's heart was hardened" (Ex. 7:13)? [5] Is this to be our interpretation, that "Pharaoh hardened his heart" means that God hardened Pharaoh's heart? Your interpretation is certainly more unreasonable than this: that God hardened the heart of Pharaoh, and this means God permitted Pharaoh to be hardened in his heart naturally, because Pharaoh refused to obey him.

They ask a similar question concerning these words: "Today, if you hear his voice, do not harden your hearts" (Heb. 3:7–8). Were you to interpret this as "God is not willing to harden your hearts," it would be absurd because he commands one man what is the work of God alone. For if the work of God is to harden the heart, man is not able to command his heart, much less to make it hard or not to make it hard. It is no more possible for man to obey than it is possible for him to add one cubit to his stature or to subtract one.

AGAINST THE TENTH ARTICLE

Article 10: Satan is a liar by the command of God.

Against your tenth article, your calumniators argue: if Satan is a liar by the command of God, to be a liar is just and Satan is just. If it is just to command a lie (which is certainly true, if Calvin speaks the truth), then to obey a lie is just, for obedience should be considered simply from the justice of the command. Again, as it is unjust to obey an unjust command, it is just to obey a just command. What if Calvin said, Satan is not a liar obediently; that is, he does

---

[5]Compare Ex. 8:15, "Pharaoh . . . hardened his heart and would not listen to them, as the LORD had said."

not obey God when he lies? We respond by using Calvin's own words, that the lie is from the command of God and that to lie is to be obedient. Likewise, Satan is obedient when he disobediently lies, since God commanded Satan not to be obedient but to lie.

AGAINST THE ELEVENTH ARTICLE

Article 11: God grants the will to perform evil. Furthermore, he prompts perverse and dishonest affections, not just permissively, but effectually, in order to further his own glory.

Against the eleventh article your calumniators declare that Calvin divides God and that this is the work of the Devil according to the testimony of Scripture. Now, truly, if God prompts perverse and shameful affections and nevertheless commands us to resist perverse affections, then he commands us to resist him, and he himself is contrary. "Every good gift and every perfect gift is from above, coming down from the Father of lights" (James 1:17).

Now, are perverse affections good gifts? Does darkness descend from the Father of lights (for perverse affections are certainly dark)? For I am not appealing to the Father of darkness. James plainly writes that no one is tempted by God but is tempted by his own lust (1:13). However, to prompt perverse affections is to tempt. And even though you add that God does this for his own glory, your calumniators say that this is ridiculous. He is not in the habit of gaining his glory from a lie. Nebuchadnezzar experienced the justice and power of God; on account of his own pride he was changed into a brute nature. He granted glory to God, for the same God who is perceiving and judging is just.

God desires to be praised by all the nations. "Praise the

LORD, all nations!" (Ps. 117:1). He requires, therefore, that all nations might be able to learn and, moreover, to praise him because of what he might do. Nevertheless, no nation at any time will recognize it as just for a man to be punished on account of the same affections that God himself prompts. For instance, we ask this: if God punishes us because we have beards, is it not doing us an injustice when he himself prompts us to have beards, and so the beard is not our choice? What bearded one might be able to praise him at any time? Suppose that Calvin said that this is the secret judgment of God that is unknown to us? We respond that it is indeed secret to God and unknown to us. Whereas that God keeps justice is well known to us, and it is to be made well known in the gospel. It is in accordance with what is being made known in the gospel (as Paul taught) and not in accordance to the secret judgment of Calvin that God will judge the world. However, the judgment will reach all people, the pious as well as the impious. Obviously all the pious and impious will consider it fair. Those who did not obey the truth, the truth that is not secret (the truth according to Calvin) but revealed (the truth according to the gospel), will be punished. Those who obeyed will receive mercy. "For the wrath of God is revealed from heaven against all ungodliness and unrighteousness of men, who by their unrighteousness suppress the truth" (Rom. 1:18).

However if Calvin's thoughts are true, the wrath of God is against all the innocent. If God prompts perverse affections and then he flies into a rage, he hates the same people before the perverse affections arise, for to prompt perverse affections is the work of hatred. Therefore, he hates the innocent. For men are innocent before the perverse affections arise. Accordingly, sin is from perverse affections, even more, sin *is* perverse affection.

AGAINST THE TWELFTH ARTICLE

Article 12: The impious, in their impiety, produce more of God's work than their own.

Concerning the twelfth article your calumniators ask: if this really is true, then God rages against the good, for if impiety is the work of God, impiety is good because all the works of God are good. Again, if impiety is good, then necessarily piety is evil because it is contrary to impiety. It will therefore follow that when Holy Scripture declares, "Hate evil, and love good" (Amos 5:15), we are commanded to love impiety and hate piety. In addition, they say that this article smacks of an ignorant libertinism. They are astonished at you, for you are hostile toward the Libertines.

AGAINST THE THIRTEENTH AND FOURTEENTH ARTICLES

Article 13: From the perspective of God we sin necessarily, whether we sin on account of our own purpose or by accident.

Article 14: Whatever perversions men perpetrate by their own will, those also proceed from the will of God.

Against these articles your calumniators argue: if we sin necessarily, all admonitions are in vain, and Jeremiah vainly declares among the people, "Behold, I set before you the way of life and the way of death. He who stays in this city shall die by the sword, by famine, and by pestilence, but he who goes out and surrenders to the Chaldeans who are besieging you shall live" (Jer. 21:8–9). I repeat that they declare this is in vain if it is as impossible for the Chaldeans to change as it is for them to swallow a mountain. What if Calvin says that the commands are displayed for the reason that men might be inexcusable? We reply that this is futile. For if you command your son to eat a rock, and he does not do it, he is no more inexcusable after the command than he was before. It is just as if God commands me, "Do not steal," and then I steal necessarily. I am not more able to abstain from stealing than I am able to eat a rock. I am not more inexcusable after the command than I was before, and I am not more excusable before the command than after it.

In short, if these words of Calvin's are true, then man is inexcusable even before the commands are given. It necessarily follows that the commandments produce nothing, when they are intended to render you inexcusable. If an impious person is reprobated before he commits impiety, that is, before he is born, from eternity he therefore sins necessarily. He is already inexcusable and condemned before receiving the command from God. This is contrary to all things concerning the law, God, and man. The law condemns man after he commits impiety. But according to Calvin, all men are condemned both before committing impiety and also on account of the act.

According to Calvin, God condemns and reprobates impiety before it happens, even before the impiety exists or men sin. Because he condemns before men sin, he forces men to sin so that it appears that he is just to condemn.

Finally, Calvin, they contrast the doctrine of your God and of their God in this way.

THE NATURE OF THE FALSE GOD

Your false God is slow to mercy and quick to wrath. He created the largest part of the world for perdition. He predestined them not only to damnation, but even to the cause of their damnation. He has also decreed from eternity both willing and causing them to sin necessarily, so that neither thefts, nor adultery, nor murder are committed unless by God's will and instigation.

He prompts even perverse and shameful affections, not only permissively but effectively, and hardens men's hearts. Therefore, while men are living in impiety they are doing the work of God and not their own, and they are unable to do otherwise. He causes Satan to be a liar, so that Satan is not the source of his own actions and the father of lies. But the God of Calvin is the father of lies who evidently governs sometimes by what he says and at other times by his secret promptings.

THE NATURE OF THE TRUE GOD

Whereas the God that reason, nature, and Holy Scripture teach is plainly contrary to the false God. He is quick to mercy and slow to wrath. He created man in his own image and his likeness, the first man by whom all men are born. He created them to be placed in paradise and to be given a blessed life. This God wills that all men might be saved and that no one would perish. For this reason he sent his Son into the world so that his righteousness might superabound wherever sin abounds. For the light of his righteousness illuminates all men who come in this world, and he calls aloud, "Come to me, all who labor and are heavy laden and I will give you rest" (Matt. 11:28). This God prompts good and honorable affections, and he liberates man from sinning necessarily. (Men sin because they cast themselves into impiety by their own disobedience.) He also heals all sickness and disease among the people. He never denies any one at any time who asks for kindness. In fact, the true God comes so that he might destroy the work of Calvin's God and cast him out.

Now these two Gods are by nature contrary to one

another; therefore, they bear sons that are contrary to one another. Those from the unmerciful God are proud, cruel, envious, bloodthirsty, calumnious, counterfeit, carrying one thing in their heart and another thing in their mouth, impatient, malicious, seditious, contentious, ambitious, avaricious, and love pleasure rather than God. In a word, they are full of perverse and shameful affections, which their father has prompted in them. But the other God begets men who are merciful, modest, gentle, benevolent, beneficent, abhorring the shedding of blood, open, speaking the truth out of the abundance of their heart, long suffering, kind, peaceful and making peace, abhorring quarrels and strife, despising their own dignity and honor, who love God more than pleasure. In one word, they are full of honest affections, which their father prompted in them.

Calvin, these are the arguments that your adversaries present concerning your doctrine. They warn all men to judge your doctrine by its fruit. Moreover, they declare that you and your disciples bear much fruit for your God. Most of your disciples are contentious, desiring vengeance, tenacious in remembering injury, full of vices that your God prompts. If anyone responds to these accusations by saying that they are not defects from your doctrine that is sound and does not beget this kind of men, your calumniators respond that your doctrine does beget this kind of men. They argue that this is evident from the fact that so many, who were less evil before, became men of this kind when they submitted to your doctrine. Now, those who believe in the true doctrine of Christ are rendered better men, but they affirm that through your doctrine these men manifestly deteriorate. In addition, when you all profess to have a sound doctrine, they respond that you are not to be believed.

Your God often says one thing and then thinks and wills another. You are truly to be feared since you imitate your God, doing what he does, and so deceiving men.

To be truthful, I once favored your doctrine, Calvin, and even though I did not sufficiently understand it, I nevertheless defended it. I attributed so much to your authority, believing that anyone thinking contrary to you to be in sin. But now having heard the arguments of your adversaries, I have nothing to respond to them. Your disciples attempt to respond by favoring those who hold to your doctrine. They confidently boast in the truth. In fact, when they encounter your adversaries, they stagger and seek protection from your books, but what they find there is weak and ineffective because your reasoning is obscure and crude. Immediately after any book of yours drops from your disciple's hand, your reasoning disappears from their memory and they are not able to convince your adversaries, whereas the arguments of your adversaries are public, sharp, easily committed to memory, and so understood by those who cannot read (the majority of those who follow Christ). So, most of your disciples depend upon your authority more than they do upon reason. And when your disciples discover that they cannot defeat your adversaries, they hold them to be heretics and obstinate. They abstain from their fellowship and warn everyone everywhere to abstain.

I honestly think we should pay attention to what is taught, not to who taught it. I judge that all opinions should be heard and tested, and then the one that is best will be upheld. Calvin, if you have arguments that are true, open, and firm, by which your adversaries might be refuted, produce them in public so that you might defend the truth. You know what is written: "I will give you a mouth and wisdom, which none of your adversaries will be able to withstand or contradict" (Luke 21:15). Wherever I am able to find the truth, I am ready to obey it and to exhort others to walk according to it.

If you have perhaps erred (for we are all men), I ask you, Calvin, to give glory to God. That will be more advantageous for you than to persist in this error. I hope that you might not be angry on account of this letter. If you are just and true, it will not seem fearful. First, it is in fact to your advantage that you might be admonished by it, and second, if you understand (as you say) that all things happen by necessity, you must also believe that this letter was written by me necessarily. Farewell.

JOHN CALVIN'S

RESPONSE

JOHN CALVIN'S
RESPONSE

I am neither ignorant of the fact that there are many adversaries against my doctrine, nor am I surprised by it. There is nothing new to Christ, under whose authority I fight. Many babblers have always made a noise against him. I grieve over this only on account of the fact that through my side the Holy One—the immortal, and truth of God—is being pierced, he who ought to be admired and adored reverently by the whole world. Yet, since I see that this doctrine has, from the beginning, been subject to many accusations from the wicked, and Christ himself, because the heavenly Father decreed so, must be the mark of contradiction, those who are to uphold this doctrine are likewise to be patient. Nevertheless, no poisonous bites of the wicked will cause me to regret the doctrine at any time. I certainly stand firm in the conviction that its authority and source are from God. I have accomplished so much in so many contests that God has brought me into that I am not in the least frightened by your futile clamoring.

Indeed, concerning you, a teacher who has been bewitched, he restrains you in private. This provides some comfort for me—you are not to be ungrateful toward the kindness of a man who has assisted you more than you deserve without at the same time revealing your grievous impiety toward God. Indeed, for you academics, there is not a more pleasing sport than overthrowing whatever the souls of men are assured of by asking questions of this kind. These doubts that you hurl against the secret providence of God are delightful to you. This is only too clear from your pen, however you might attempt to disguise yourself. But I now summon you and all your cronies to the tribunal from which, in the future, the only judge of heaven is to breathe from his mouth his crushing sentence. He will effectively and powerfully strike you down—the impudent one. I am confident in the fact that your ridicule will soon become offensive to our honorable and wise readers, even though you are secretly pleased with yourself.

You force out of me a refutation to your treatise that you secretly sent from Paris to the city in Switzerland. If I had remained ignorant of what you have written, your venom might be spread far and wide without remedy. While you imitate some zeal for acquiring knowledge, I cannot understand the reason why I am unaware of your name; that is, unless you knew that I have something on hand that would immediately abolish you and your followers' credit. Nevertheless, with careful study you can be identified. I can judge who you are from your writings.

Whether you wrote by your own hand or you dictated your madness to a Scottish preacher[1] so that it could be carried to Paris, it does not matter to me—but it was certainly unlawful to publish it here. If only this book had another author or you yourself were another man. But you will never be that other man until you taste genuine virtue and love. Although you have always spoken to me with respect, it is not difficult to recognize that your nature is still given to cavilling. You even promote this vice with childish frivolities. I have striven to correct you, but it has been in vain because these perverse

---

[1] This person's identity is otherwise unknown.

affections are a part of your nature. By telling tasteless jokes you long to be praised for sharpness by those without life. Nor is it right that you hide behind the example of Socrates, who you say was accustomed to attacking things said against him with jesting.[2] For that man excelled in many noble virtues, but this one vice stained him, the same vice which you emulate and is no less dangerous than greed.

You ask me to write a refutation for you that can be understood by the people. Indeed, I do what I can to accommodate myself by bringing forth simple and pure teaching to suit the capacity of the most elementary. But if you allow no other form of reasoning except what an earthly man recognizes, then by such arrogance and disdain you deny yourself access to the very doctrine the knowledge of which is only possible to someone with a reverential spirit. I am not ignorant of the mockery that comes from you and those like you, with which you harass the mysteries of God. Everything loses its authority and grace if it does not satisfy your reason.

For what reason am I compelled to provide a refutation against anyone who chooses to roar against me? Not even Socrates, whose name you falsely hide behind, would suffer himself to be imposed upon by such a demand. I have little desire for thoughtless imitation, but if there was someone in this age, or any other, who constantly opposed wickedness by refuting his calumniators, even those who are malevolent and unjust to me would honor me for this kind of work. Your barking is less tolerable so long as you trample on my labors in your blind and shameless attacks. For you ask me to carry out a task that has been accomplished three or four times already.

You say that those who fight against me have one article

---

[2]Castellio does not appear to allude to Socrates anywhere in the Fourteen Articles. Perhaps Calvin is recalling an earlier writing.

that is so powerful that no arguments from my books thus far published have been able to refute it. This article, you say, is the subject of predestination or fate. If only you might display your wisdom by inquiring modestly or at least by disputing generously. Instead, you disregard decency and extinguish the light by confusing things that are opposite. Fate, named by the Stoics, is that which is necessary from the various and complicated labyrinth of causes that in some manner restricts God himself.[3]

By contrast with this, I define predestination, in line with what Holy Scripture teaches, as the free counsel of God by which he governs the human race and every single part of the universe according to his immense wisdom and incomprehensible justice. Now you are prevented from seeing anything in perfect light by your depravity of mind, your appetite for being quarrelsome, and the diabolical pride that has blinded you. Yet readers with eyes to see the distinction between fate and predestination perceive the fairness of your judgments. You may have concluded, if you had not been so disinclined to examine my books, how much that word *fate* displeases me. You would have been able to know, indeed you would have read, that the same disagreeable and spiteful objections were formerly used against Augustine by impure and worthless men like yourself. Also, by that same pious and holy doctor there is a brief response set forth, which would suffice as a defense for my cause today.[4]

---

[3]Here and elsewhere in his writings Calvin makes a sharp distinction between Stoic fate and predestination. Stoic fatalism is a complex cosmic causal system to which even God or "the gods" are subject. Some Stoics were astrological fatalists. Calvin's chief objection is that such a causal is not the work of a transcendent creator. He offers this critique of it in a number of places; e.g., in *Concerning the Eternal Predestination of God*, trans. J. K. S. Reid (London: James Clarke, 1961), 170, and *Institutes* I.16.8, and of astrological fatalism in *A Warning Against Judicial Astrology and Other Prevalent Curiosities* (1549), trans. Mary Potter (*Calvin Theological Journal*, 1983).

[4]*Against Two Letters of the Pelagians*, bk. 2, chap. 6, 11–12; *The City of God*, v.9.3.

In this article, which you say may be extracted from my books, my method is the same as with the author of happy memory.[5] The malevolent know that this is not a popular doctrine. Those with the purpose of increasing hatred boast of articles that are partly false and partly true so that the uninformed are not able to make a well-balanced judgment. Even though, at first sight, many supposed these to be extracts from his writings, yet he complains that these are falsely attributed to him.[6] They either with great diligence combined broken sentences or by their trickery they corrupted his pious and righteous declarations by changing a few words so that they might cause offense to the simpleminded.

You boast that you are deploying these articles from my books, but they are absolutely of the same kind as Augustine's. Even were I to remain silent, honest and sincere readers would discover this. It would not be troublesome to compare your impure calumnies with my doctrine. And indeed I maintain this to be of the utmost importance: you neither behave straightforwardly nor act generously so long as you do not refer to the relevant passage, so that intelligent readers could read what you have alleged to be my doctrine for themselves.

What could be more unjust, when I have published so many books, to vaguely recite a collection of fourteen articles from the fifty books I have written? It would certainly have been better, if there was a drop of honesty in you, either to record my sentences verbatim or, if you saw something dangerous, to warn your readers of which parts they should beware. By blackening all my known works as improper, you would destroy their reputation. Whatever is in my books that is without any offense you spitefully distort and so ren-

---

[5] Augustine.
[6] E.g., *Retractions*. II.33A.

der yourself offensive. I do not condemn the prudence of Augustine when he opposed the cleverness and wickedness of his enemies by tempering his response so that he might avoid being hated. But I believe it to be more useful, frankly to refute your abuse than to give the slightest hint that I am turning my back on your accusations.

Article 1: By his bare and pure will God creates the greater part of the world for destruction.

You take hold of the first article, "By his bare and pure will God creates the greater part of the world for destruction." All this about "the greater part of the world" and the "bare and pure will" is fictitious and the product of your malicious imagination. Though it is true that from the beginning God determined the future of the entire human race, this way of talking about the end of creation being eternal destruction occurs nowhere in my writings. Like a pig you dig up doctrine that smells sweet so that you might discover something offensive instead. Though the will of God is to me the greatest cause, I still everywhere teach that where his counsel and work are not apparent, it is hidden in him. Nothing is decreed that is not just and wise. Therefore, I not only repudiate but detest the schoolmen talking nonsense about absolute power, because they separate his justice from his supreme authority.

Now see, you dog, what you accomplish by your violent barking. I subject the human race to God's decision, and I boldly affirm that nothing is decreed by him without the best reason. If today we are unaware of that reason it will be made known in the last day. When you force on me this "bare and pure will," you shamelessly reproach me with what I publicly reject in a hundred or more places. At the same time,

I acknowledge that this is my doctrine—that Adam fell not only by the permission of God but by his secret counsel and that all his descendents are fallen, being dragged into eternal destruction.

I see that both these doctrines are displeasing because to you they are repugnant both to nature and to Scripture. You prove that it is contrary to nature by arguing that all creatures naturally love their offspring. Likewise God, who inspired the same kind of affections in brute animals, must not love men less because they are his offspring. Truly, this reasoning is too crass. Whatever you discern in the cow and the donkey you find the same in God, who is the Creator of nature, as if he were confined by the same laws that he proclaimed for his creatures. He inspired each with a desire to procreate so that all animals might give birth to their kind. Now, demand of him why he was content with himself from all eternity to keep his power as if it were sterile and not procreate like the creatures he inspired. He must always be like himself. If you therefore are the judge, it must follow that he violated the order of nature as long as he preferred to be without offspring rather than to reveal his fruitfulness. If wild beasts fight to the death for their offspring, how is it that God allows young infants to be mangled and devoured by tigers, bears, lions, or wolves? Is it because his arm is too short to stretch forth so that he might protect his children?

You see how broad my field could be if it suited me to go into every detail about how you play the fool. But this alone is sufficient for me, that there are enough testimonies pointing toward God's love for the entire human race to prove that all who will die in a state of ingratitude are guilty. Nor is this any different from his special love with which he draws out a few whom he esteems enough to be chosen from the many. Certainly when he formerly adopted the race of Abraham, by that act he gave a public testimony that he does not love every member of the human race equally. So when he rejected Esau and preferred his younger brother Jacob, he provided a clear demonstration of his free love. Whom he chooses, he pursues with this love. Moses declared that one nation is loved by God and the others are rejected. The prophets everywhere affirm that the only reason Judah was preeminent was that God loved them freely. Will you deny that he is God because you do not find any similarity between him and a tiger or a bear? And Christ addressing a little flock, not the entire human race or even the entire Jewish race, did not in vain declare, "Fear not, little flock, for it is your Father's good pleasure to give you the kingdom" (Luke 12:32). Truly, only those whom he restores to himself in his only-begotten Son will experience the Father's love in hope of eternal life.

If it is your practice to subject God to the laws of nature, you condemn him for injustice because on account of one man's sin we are all implicated into his guilt and eternal death. One man sinned; therefore, all men are dragged to punishment. Not only this, but from one contact with sin, all men commit sin, so that all are born being infected with a corrupt and fatal fault. Noble critic, what do you have to say to this? Will you condemn God for cruelty because for one man's sin he casts all his offspring into destruction? Though Adam destroyed himself and his offspring, it is necessary to ascribe the corruption and guilt to God's secret judgment. For one man's sin is nothing to us unless the Celestial Judge sentences us to eternal destruction for it.

See how, to conceal your error, you cite passages of

Isaiah and adopt a strained interpretation. It is incredible that the church of God, while in Babylonian captivity, was not deprived of one child. Rather, having become barren, she should have recovered fresh vigor in order to be more fruitful than before. Thus God speaks, "Am I, by whose strength women give birth, not also able to produce offspring?"[7] Under this pretext you force God to dress himself with the affections of creatures. You audaciously reason that because God fashions his creatures to love their offspring, he too must love his own offspring. Even if this were conceded, it does not follow that he must love them all in the same way. Besides, this does not hinder him as the just judge from rejecting those whom, like the perfect Father, he pursues with love and grace.

Again you argue that to create is a work of love and not of hatred, and therefore God creates out of love and not out of hatred. You do not recognize that in Adam all men are hateful toward God; nevertheless, his love shines in creation. Therefore, anyone with mediocre judgment and gifted with impartiality will recognize as frivolous what you think is worthy of praise. It is not for me to refute by writing what you next expound but for the judge to punish with the sword. That men are born into misery is public knowledge. For what reason is this fact to be reckoned to be an invention of my books? From what kind of situation does this arise, that man is not only born into temporal misery but also, being guilty, into eternal death, if it is not because God has cast us into the common guilt for one man's sin?

In this miserable ruin of the human race it is not my sentences that are being judged but God's revealed work. You do not hesitate to vomit out sacrilegious noises such

---

[7] The likely reference is Isaiah 66:9: "'Shall I bring to the point of birth and not cause to bring forth?' says the LORD, 'Shall I, who cause to bring forth, shut the womb?' says your God."

that God is worse than any wolf if he wills to create man for misery. Some are born blind, others deaf, yet others horribly deformed. If you were the judge, God would be cruel because he would afflict his offspring with great disadvantage before they come to see the light of day. In the future you will realize how much better for you to have seen nothing than to have been so attentive when examining the mysteries of God. You certainly accuse God of injustice; you even call him a monster if he raises the human race differently from how we raise our own children. Why then did he create some slow, some stupid, and others fools? Just as the fauns and satyrs of Jewish fables stated that their god was not able to complete his work because he was prevented by the arrival of the Sabbath day, and they were not acquitted of guilt, will you speak so foolishly as to assert that those who are abnormal escape from his hands?[8]

It is preferable that such a sad spectacle would teach us reverence and modesty rather than arouse a quarrelsome sense in our minds concerning the Creator of heaven and the earth. If I happen to meet a fool, it admonishes me to contemplate how God could have created me. Just as many are stupid and slow in the world, so God has displayed to me just as many spectacles in which his power is revealed. To me this is no less terrifying than wonderful. But in truth you permit yourself to babble against him, so that he is worse than a wolf because he looks after his creation with such malice.

---

[8]Compare Calvin on Gen. 2:3: "Here the Jews, in their usual method, foolishly trifle, saying, that God being anticipated in his work by the last evening, left certain animals imperfect, of which kind are fauns and satyrs, as though he had been one of the ordinary class of artificers who have need of time. Ravings so monstrous prove the authors of them to have been delivered over to a reprobate mind, as a dreadful example of the wrath of God." According to A. N. S. Lane, Calvin's source for this Jewish tradition and other Jewish material in the *Genesis Commentary* is Sebastian Munster's Latin Bible of 1534–1535. (A. N. S. Lane, *John Calvin: Student of the Church Fathers* [Edinburgh: T&T Clarke, 1999], 217 fn. 63). Calvin's *Genesis Commentary* was published in 1554.

Christ declares that God, who is good, acts more kindly toward his sons than do men who are evil.[9] Before you please yourself with your reasoning, it must be proved that all men are equally God's sons. It is commonly understood that all men lost their eternal life in Adam, whereas adoption is certainly a special grace. It follows that those who are haters of God, or rather are hated by God, are alienated from God. All the testimonies of Scripture that you cite are like darts flung blindly by the hand of a madman. God saw what he had made, and it was very good. Hence you deduce that man is very good, from which you further infer that God is unjust if he created something good for destruction. In what manner man was created with an upright nature I have explained more than sufficiently in many places.[10] Certainly man was not better than the Devil before he (the Devil) fell from his integrity. Now, if I were to concede to you that man as well as apostate angels were created for prosperity, and also that with respect to their future defection they were destined for destruction, what will you conclude from this? We will look later, at the proper place, at the matter of the permission of God.

Now, if you object that the foreknowledge of God is not the cause of evil, I only ask you this: if God foresaw the destruction of both the Devil and man before he created them, why did he not quickly apply the remedy in order to prevent their fall? Immediately from the beginning of the world, Satan alienated himself from the hope of salvation. Similarly man, as soon as he was created, destroyed himself and his posterity in the deadly fall. If the preservation of both was in the hand of God, why did he suffer them to die? Even more, why did God

---

[9]Matt. 7:11.
[10]This is an allusion to the view that while Adam and Eve were created sinless, they nevertheless had the liability to fall (*Inst.* I.15.8).

not construct man with at least a moderate degree of constancy and protection? However much you might go round in circles and change, I keep to this principle: however much man was created weak and capable of destruction, this weakness was a great blessing. This is because he was taught shortly after his destruction that nothing is secure or steadfast except God himself. Hence, it is also concluded that your ranting about man being created for happiness[11] is considered out of order and not thought through. Therefore when I acknowledge that nothing in man is contrary to salvation, you believe that all men are predestined to salvation by God's secret counsel.

Let me briefly repeat this in other words. If merely the sound human nature that Adam was given at the beginning of his creation is observed, then man is created for salvation because nothing is found there that might cause death. But if we were to search into the secret providence of God, we would be met with that profound abyss that ought to drive us to admiration. Indeed, if you had been given even a small appetite for piety, you would easily acknowledge that the passage "and it was very good"[12] was not about man's perfect state, as if the Holy Spirit declared that nothing is missing in the excellency of mankind. It was said in order to take away your opportunity, and that of those like you, to roar against God because you deny that it was good for man to be created under this law.

Adam immediately corrupted the whole world by his fall, yet God proclaimed that this plan was pleasing to him, and therefore it is most righteous. So that you might come to a better understanding of Moses, he did not assert that man is just or perfect. Instead, in order that he might stop your barking, he

---

[11]The Latin *salutur* can mean either "happiness" or "salvation."
[12]Gen. 1:31.

teaches that the order of the world as a whole was established by God so that nothing could be more proper. Consequently, when he spoke of the many individual works of God, he said, "God saw everything that he had made, and behold, it was very good." Concerning man's specific excellency he affirms nothing. But when he narrates his creating, he only reveals so much in general: "Whatever God has made, it is very good." Under this declaration is undoubtedly comprehended what Solomon says: "The wicked are created for the day of trouble" (Prov. 16:4). The sum is this: that although man was created with a natural goodness, this righteousness, which was frail and perishable, is not at odds with the predestination of God. The result is that man was destroyed by his own guilt even though his created nature was pure and he was ordained to be regarded as excellent because he was created for salvation. Therefore, you wrongly and foolishly advance the idea that God creates in order to destroy what is good, even though it is clear that man dies for his own sin and (that) he suffered a just condemnation because of his guilt. Later on we shall see more clearly how these two truths agree with one another.

You object, "God has no pleasure in the death of the wicked" (Ezek 33:11). But you should pay attention to what follows in the writings of the prophet. Truly God invites all men to repentance; therefore, all might return to the road where he offers pardon. Now, what we must here consider is whether the conversion that God requires is according to man's free choice or is a truly unique gift from God. Therefore, insofar as all men are exhorted to repent, the prophet rightly denies that God wills the death of the sinner. Why does God not convert everyone to himself equally? The reason is in the hands of God's secret will. You are in the habit of quoting from Paul—"God desires the salvation of all men" (1 Tim. 2:4)—arguing that he desires no one to suffer death. I have made your error in understanding this passage clear elsewhere.[13] It is absolutely certain that Paul is not speaking in this verse of each single man, but he is referring to the orders and classes of vocations. He commanded prayers to be uttered for the king, for leaders, and for all who bear a civil office. But for everyone who bears the sword, just as many are professed enemies of the church. So it would have seemed absurd for the church to pray for their salvation. Paul, anticipating that this might cause offence, extends the grace of God even to the enemies of the church.

Perhaps more to the point are the words of Peter, "God does not wish that any should perish, but that all should reach repentance" (2 Pet. 3:9). If there was any ambiguity in the first clause, it is clarified by the explanation in the second clause. Of course, to the extent that God wills all to be received by repentance, he wills that no one perishes. But it is necessary to come in order to be received. Throughout Scripture the Spirit of God proclaims that this first comes from God, that until men are drawn by God they will remain enslaved to their carnal disobedience. If the smallest amount of judgment remained in you, you might at last realize that there is a difference between these two—hearts of men are made from stone into flesh so that they are to be displeased with themselves and to ask God for his favor and to pray for his mercy; and after which they are changed and are received into grace. God declares that both of these things are gifts from his kindness; he gives us hearts that we might repent and he graciously forgives those who ask.

---

[13]See, e.g., *Institutes* III. 24.16, an altered text of the 1539 edition. Also *Commentaries on the First Epistle to Timothy* (1556) and *Concerning the Eternal Predestination of God*, 109.

Unless God were prepared to receive those who truly ask for his mercy, he would not declare, "Return to me, says the LORD of Hosts, and I will return to you" (Zech 1:3). Truly, if repenting was in the power of man's will, Paul would not have said, "God may perhaps grant them repentance" (2 Tim. 2:25). Indeed, unless God himself exhorts all men to repentance by his own voice, and leads the elect by the secret stirring of his Spirit, Jeremiah would not have said, "Bring me back that I may be restored, for you are the LORD my God. For after I had turned away, I relented" (Jer. 31:18–19).[14]

If there is any modesty in a dog, this solution ought have been known to you from my many writings. It is permitted for you to reject this, but there will not be any more support for you from Paul than from Ezekiel. How God wills every man to salvation is not to be meticulously debated, because these two invariably go together—salvation and the knowledge of truth. Now answer this: if God had willed his truth to be made known to all men, why is it that so many nations have never received his pure truth since the first proclamation of the gospel? Also, why has he not enlightened every eye equally, since the internal illumination of the Spirit, who only condescends to a few, is necessary for faith?

This knot is also for you to untie. Since no one comes near to God unless the secret influence of the Spirit draws him, why are not all men without discrimination drawn, if God wills all to salvation? For from his discrimination it certainly is to be concluded that God has a particular secret way in which many are excluded from salvation. How the mercy of God extends unto the thousandth generation you will never perceive as long as you are swollen with the

---

[14]Calvin's translation states, "After I was turned, I repented."

pride that makes you dull. For no such mercy is promised that would thoroughly abolish the curse under which the entire race of Adam was crushed, but a promise has come to the unworthy that continuously breaks through and overcomes every obstacle.

This God passed by many sons of Abraham when he chose one son, Isaac. Also, when the twin sons of Isaac were born, God willed to rest his mercy on the one son, Jacob. Yet however much God makes known a proof of his anger toward many, it nevertheless remains true that he is inclined to good and to be slow to anger. In his longsuffering he sustains the condemned, and this clearly reflects his goodness without any question.

Now see how all your frivolous deceptions, from which I easily free myself, ensnare you. When making the mercy of God superior to his wrath, you will have more to be chosen for salvation than for destruction. And even if I were to concede this much to you, God is still no less unjust for those who are chosen for destruction, if your calumniators are to be believed. Unless God loved all his offspring, you will still pronounce him to be worse than a wolf. If there was just one against whom God exercises his wrath, how will he clear himself from the crime of cruelty? Nor will you accept that the causes of wrath are in man himself. When comparing both wrath and mercy, you contend for the greatness of one more than the other, as if by choosing more to salvation God might prove himself to be merciful. Rather, God commends his grace to us in a boundlessly different way, by forgiving so many and such varied sins, and by striving with the obstinate malice of men while their sin reaches its culmination.

Article 2: God not only predestined Adam to damnation but also predestined the causes of his damnation, whose fall he not only foresaw, but by his secret and eternal decree he ordained that he would perish. In order that this would come about in due time, God provided the apple for the purpose of the fall.

You are exactly the same man in the second article as you were before. Provide, if you can, the passage from my writings where I teach that the fruit was placed before Adam by God in order to cause his fall. Here is certainly the source of your popularity—you confuse the minds of the simple with lies, in case they might rise to the truth that is far from the common understanding of the carnal. But for fear that I appear to quarrel over words, I do confess to writing as follows: the fall of Adam was not by accident but was ordained by the secret decree of God. In so far as you abruptly call this the doctrine of the Devil, you certainly regard yourself as a judge of great authority. You hope to be able to destroy with one insult what I have demonstrated by many arguments of sound reasoning. You require us to produce a testimony from Scripture proving that Adam was not able to fall without the secret decree of God. But if you had read just a few pages of my works with attention, what occurs everywhere would not have escaped you, which is that everything is governed by God's secret counsel.

You add foreknowledge to God so that he is idle, watching the life of men from heaven. However, God's own hand is at the helm of the entire world, so that he never allows a separation between his power and his prescience. This is certainly not my reasoning alone, but Augustine's: if God foresaw what he did not will to be, then he does not have the highest authority. Therefore, he established what will come about in the future, because nothing happens unless he wills that it happens.[15] If you judge that this is absurd, you will fall back on your own fiction—that in every event of evil he has an obligation to provide the remedy because it is in his hand. This is despite the fact that it is clear he did not do as you demand. God foresaw the fall of Adam. He had the resources in his own hands to prevent the fall, but he was not willing. Why did he not will it? It is not possible to produce any other reason except that he directed his will another way. If you allow yourself to quarrel with God, then accuse him as well, because he prepared man, being born with frailty for ruin.

You say that Adam fell by his free will. I reply, he would not have fallen if he had possessed the needed fortitude and perseverance that God provides for his elect when he wills to keep their integrity. This is certain, that unless virtue is provided from heaven each new moment, because we are fallen we would be ruined a thousand times over. Whomever God elects, he supports with an unconquerable fortitude for perseverance. Would this not have been provided for Adam, if he had willed him to remain alive?

This is certain: it is necessary either to be silent or to confess with Solomon, "The LORD has made everything for its purpose, even the wicked for the day of trouble" (Prov. 16:4). If this "absurdity" offends you, you must recognize that it is not in vain that Scripture repeats so many times that the judgments of God are a profound mystery. If it is lawful for the incomprehensible counsel of God to be measured by the little

---

[15]This citation from Augustine could be a paraphrase of any one of several passages, e.g., "And this certainly is not true, if God has ever willed anything that He has not performed; and, still worse, if it was the will of man that hindered the Omnipotent from doing what He pleased. Nothing, therefore, happens but by the will of the Omnipotent, He either permitting it to be done, or Himself doing it" (trans. J. F. Shaw, *Enchiridion* 95, in *A Select Library of the Nicene and Post-Nicene Fathers of the Christian Church*, vol. 3, ed. Philip Schaff [Grand Rapids, Eerdmans, 1978], 267). See also *The City of God*, vols. 9–11, XXII. 2.

measure of our senses, Moses would have declared in vain, "The secret things belong to the LORD our God, but the things that are revealed belong to us and to our children forever, that we may do all the words of this law" (Deut. 29:29).

You demand that I demonstrate the places in Scripture that establish that God did not prevent the fall of Adam because he did not will to do so. As if this one memorable response of God was not sufficient proof: "I will have mercy on whom I will have mercy," from which Paul concludes that all do not receive mercy because God does not will it (Ex. 33:19; Rom. 9:15). Certainly, these words, which need no interpreter, clearly declare that God is not confined by any law to the effect that all men equally deserve mercy. Rather, he is his own Lord, able to bestow favor on whomever he desires and to disregard others. It is certain that at that time God is the same as he was when the prophet asserted, "He does according to his will."[16] And if he permits unwillingly, then you must declare that Satan was the victor in the contest, and you must also declare that there are two ruling principles, like the Manichees.[17]

Paul likewise pleads this efficient cause, for he does not thoughtlessly compare God to a potter, who from the same mass can freely create different vessels as he wills to mold them. Paul could have begun with sin, but he does not. Instead, he defends the free justice and the supremacy of God in the work itself. Where he certainly added that all were imprisoned under disbelief, does he declare that it came about against God's will or rather that God is the author of it? If you reply, all were condemned to unbelief as they deserved, the context

[16]Dan. 4:35.
[17]Manichaeanism, a form of Gnosticism, maintained an essentially dualistic position, holding that the cosmos is governed by two eternal principles, Light and Darkness, in perpetual conflict.

does not permit it, because Paul is discussing the secret judgments of God, and this exclamation, "Oh, the depth. etc."[18] is in conflict with your interpretation. Therefore, just as he predestined Christ in the beginning to help those who were being destroyed, so by his unsearchable counsel he decreed a way for his glory to be illumined through the fall of Adam.

Certainly I confess that where God is vindicating the free course of his mercy, he is speaking of the human race generally, which has already perished in Adam. But the same reason prevailed before the fall of Adam, that his will is alone sufficient to show mercy and he shows mercy as he desires. Further, this will depends upon no other cause; neither does it have a prior cause; but it is nevertheless still found to be the most rational and to possess the greatest equity. Now the outrageous behavior of men requires a law for bridling, but for God the rule is different. He is his own law, and his will is the rule of the highest uprightness.[19]

Article 3: The sins that are committed are not solely by God's permission, but are committed even by the very will of God. For as far as sin is concerned, it is frivolous to make a distinction between the permission and the will of God. Whoever makes this distinction wishes to please God by flattery and adulation.

The third article, no less than the others, reveals how passionately you feed upon foul objections. If it is pleasing to gnaw away at my doctrine, why did you not at least reproduce my words directly? As far as the calumny that I am now being presented with is concerned, I maintain that the distinction between permission and volition is frivolous. You oppose

---

[18]Rom. 11:33.
[19]Compare the very similar language of *Institutes* III.23.2 (trans. Henry Beveridge): "We do not imagine God to be lawless. He is a law to himself; because, as Plato says, men labouring under the influence of concupiscence need law."

what you consider to be a silly argument, but your opposition itself is thin and fallacious. You say, if everything is done by the will of God, then he wills things that are opposed to one another. For instance, you say I am a prophet of the Devil, while I maintain that I am truly his faithful servant. This appearance of a contradiction is repugnant to you, but in truth God himself, who knows within himself how to will and not will the same thing, is not slowed down by your sluggishness of mind. As often as he raises up true prophets whom he wills steadfastly and strenuously to fight to protect the doctrine of his law, false prophets arise who desire to overturn this doctrine. There must be a clash between these prophets, but God was not at odds with himself when he raised them both up.

You force the idea of God's toleration of evil upon me, yet he declares that no false prophets arise unless he ordains them in order to test his people's faith or to blind the unbelieving. "If a prophet or a dreamer of dreams rises among you," Moses says, ". . . the Lord your God is testing you" (Deut. 13:1–3). By some worthless gloss you transfer to another what Moses clearly ascribes to God. So either you must deny that God may test the hearts of his people, or you must finally recognize this clear and indubitable truth—that false prophets are the instruments of God for testing his people and that he desires to be acknowledged as the one who sends them. Ezekiel is even clearer. "And if the prophet is deceived and speaks a word, I, the Lord, have deceived that prophet" (Ezek. 14:9). You require us to rest content with mere permission, but God asserts that his will and his hand are the cause. Now reflect on which testimony is more trustworthy: either God speaking of himself by his Spirit (who is the only fountain of wisdom) or you chattering about God's hidden mysteries according to your carnal, foolish understanding. What? When God calls Satan the agent of his vengeance and gives him a public command to deceive, does this not differ from mere permission? The voice of God is clear. "Who will entice Ahab?" And there is no obscurity when he commands Satan, "You are to entice him, and you shall succeed; go out and do so" (1 Kings 22:20, 22).

I want to be clear about whether to do something is the same as to permit it. Because David secretly abused another man's wife, God declared that he would cause his wives to be dragged out in the sight of the sun for a similar disgrace in public (2 Sam. 12:11). He did not say, "I will allow it to happen," but, "I will cause it to happen." You appeal to permission in order to help God out by using an illogical defense. But when reflecting on the terrible judgment of God, David understood things differently, and exclaimed, "I am silenced because you brought it about."[20] In the same way Job blesses God when he acknowledges that he was plundered by robbers not only by the permission of God, for he openly confesses that it was God who took away what he had given.[21]

On your authority, if the same rule about permission also holds in the case of giving and receiving, then wealth is not a blessing of God but comes blindly from God's mere permission. Even though you and your followers do not stop angrily protesting against God, nevertheless God will justify himself. We reverently adore mysteries that far surpass our comprehension until a full knowledge of them shines forth when we see him face-to-face, the one who is now able to be seen only darkly, through a mirror. "Then," Augustine says, "God will be seen in the clearest light of understanding that the godly presently have

---

[20]E.g., Ps. 39:9, "I am mute; I do not open my mouth, for it is you who have done it."
[21]Job 1:21.

by faith. How certain, immutable, and effective is the will of God; how much could be done that he does not will, but nothing is willed that is not possible."[22] As far as this present article is concerned, I reply to you from the lips of the same godly writer: "These are the mighty works of God, exquisite in every way according to his will. God's works are so wonderfully wise that when angelic and human creatures sinned, that is, when they did not do what he commanded, nevertheless in the very willing of what they did, which was itself against the command of the Creator, God brought to pass what he willed."[23]

The one who is supremely good wisely uses evil for the damnation of those he justly predestines to punishment and for the salvation of those he predestined to grace. So far as men are concerned, they did what God did not will; but as far as the omnipotence of God is concerned, it was impossible for them to accomplish anything without it. So when they were acting contrary to the will of God, they were in fact accomplishing his will. Therefore, the great works of the Lord are carefully crafted in respect of all that he wills, so that in a wonderful and ineffable way nothing happens contrary to his will, even that which is contrary to his will! For nothing happens if he does not permit it, and he does not permit anything unwillingly, but willingly. Neither does his permitting an evil make that evil good, except insofar as, by his omnipotence, he brings it about that good comes from the evil.

As to the testimonies you cite, they have nothing more to do with the present issue than wine may be of use to dilute oil. Speaking to the immoral Jews through the prophet Ezekiel, God said, "Go serve every one of you his idols" (Ezek. 20:39). I reckon that this expression is certainly not a command but

---

[22]*Enchiridion*, 95.
[23]Ibid., 100.

a rejection of the impious additions by which the Jews had adulterated his worship. Now what else will you conclude from this except that God sometimes permits what he disapproves of and condemns? As if it were not evident to all that God uses the same forms of expression sometimes to command and at other times to permit. He says in the law, you will work six days. This is an act of permission, for the seventh day is consecrated for himself while the other six remain free for man. In another way he permitted the Jews to divorce their wives in a manner that he certainly did not approve. Here he indignantly gives up the double-minded and [the] faithless to the worship of idols because he does not wish his name to be profaned. But how is it that you are driven to forget that our present subject is the secret providence of God, by which he destines and directs every movement of the world for his own will according to his pleasure?

Moreover, by ignorantly and perversely corrupting another passage you reveal that to an impure and profane man there is nothing sacred. God's words are: "Because they had not obeyed my rules . . . I gave them statutes that were not good" (Ezek. 20:24–25). Here you talk nonsense: "When they were deserted by God, they fell into idolatry." Undoubtedly God means that they were sentenced to slavery by the Chaldeans, who forced them to obey their tyrannical laws. Now, the question is this: did God merely permit the Jews to be dragged into exile by the Chaldeans or did he choose them as his own arm to accomplish his purpose of chastising the sins of his people according to his will? If you still seek a pretext from the permission of God, every prophet must be consigned to the flames because they all confirm that Satan was sent by God in order to deceive and that the Chaldeans and Assyrians were sent to enslave. They declare that the same God summoned the Egyptians in order to use their service; that the Assyrians were his hired soldiers; that Nebuchadnezzar was his servant to plunder the Egyptians; that the Assyrians were the ax in his hand and the rod of his fury for the purpose of destroying Judah. [24] In order not to be accused of being longwinded I pass over numerous other accounts. It is no less than drunken recklessness when you pretend that God sends spirits of error to the unbelieving so they might believe a lie by merely permitting false teachers to exist, just as he allows the prodigal son to fall into ruin by indulging himself.

When you talk foolishly about these things, do you think those reading what you have written are so blind that they might see an absolutely different meaning in Paul's words, "God sends them a strong delusion" (2 Thess. 2:11)? There is nothing remarkable about someone babbling in such an unrestrained way, who says either that there are no divine judgments or whose contempt for the very word *judgment* is so strong. But no one with a sound mind would say that a judge has no part in weighing the wicked for punishment or that he relinquishes to others the duties of the work that is proper to his office.

Moreover, with your barking you strive to intimidate and challenge me, but this has no effect. You assert that spirits of error exist by the mere permission of God and that these spirits teach that God wills sin. Paul was reproached in the same way by men who resemble you (Rom. 3:5), and I would not feel uncomfortable to be associated with him. You argue from Zechariah that God is angry with those nations who plundered

---

[24]Examples of the sort of biblical material Calvin has in mind here are Satan as a lying spirit, 1 Kings 22:20; the Chaldeans sent to enslave, Jeremiah 21 (cf. *Institutes* I.18.1); God summoning the Egyptians, 2 Chron. 12:1–9; Nebuchadnezzar, Jeremiah 46; the Assyrians as God's hired soldiers and his ax and rod, Isa. 10:5.

the Israelites more than his anger allowed.[25] Are you so stupid to think that if he willed to chastise his people more mildly there is not enough in God for help to prohibit further injury? You will object to this being the true meaning of the words. But you are stupid three times over—nay, four times!—if you do not appreciate that God has one extraordinary way to severely test the patience of his people, while at the same time in another way he is offended by the aggression of the enemy when he sees that they have become haughty in their victory and rush into cruelty.

Indeed nothing is clearer than this—that the ways in which you play the fool cancel each other out. God either commanded or only permitted these profane nations to chastise Judah leniently. If you answer that it is a command, I maintain that without good reason these neighbors were troublesome to the wretched exiles of God. Yet if they had observed God's boundary they would have been blameless, for who would ascribe any fault to them so long as they obeyed the command of God? Yet you establish a distinction between God's permission and his command. So when the Lord commanded them to punish his people lightly, by his permission they exceeded the boundary that he had erected.[26] According to this reasoning,

---

[25]Note Calvin's comment on Zech. 1:15: "A reason also follows, *Because God was a little angry, and they helped forward the evil*; that is, they exceeded moderation. The meaning is, that the reward of cruelty would be repaid to all the enemies of the Church, because they had exercised immoderate severity, when it was God's purpose to chastise his children in a gentle and paternal manner" (*Commentaries on Zechariah*). It is interesting also that in his remarks on this verse Calvin mentions that "this place has been also laid hold of by that miscreant, who has been lately writing against God's providence, holding that the wicked become wanton by means of God's hand and power, and are not thereby restrained. But this is extremely foolish; for the Prophet here does not regard what the nations were able to do or had done; but, on the contrary, he speaks of their cruelty, that they thought that there ought to have been no end until the memory of the people had been obliterated." That is a clear reference to Castellio. The commentary on Zechariah was published in 1559.

[26]At this point Calvin moves from Zech. 1:15 to consider Castellio's reference to 2 Chron. 28:8–9, which depicts Israel as the chastiser of Judah: "The men of Israel took captive 200,000 of their relatives, women, sons, and daughters. They also took much spoil from them and brought the spoil to Samaria. But a prophet of the LORD was there, whose name was Oded: and he went out before the host that came to Samaria, and said unto them, 'Behold, because the LORD God of your fathers was wroth with Judah, he hath delivered them into your hand, but you have killed them in a rage that has reached up to heaven.'"

the Israelites are worthy of reproof because they afflicted their brothers more than the anger of God allowed. But in releasing them from being charged guilty provided that they had kept themselves within God's boundaries, your madness blinds you too much.

I shall keep returning you to this point. The Israelites were not guilty by God's permission alone, as you pretend, as they behaved extremely harshly, even fighting excessively against their brothers. You assert without hesitation that there was nothing sinful in waging war, because God was angry with the Jews and that he himself armed the Israelites so that they might carry out his command of vengeance. But I declare that they sinned in two different ways. Firstly, by their actions they showed no intention of obeying God even while they were the instruments of his judgment. Secondly, their atrocities revealed that all Israel had lost any sense of equity.

In adopting this principle you reveal a shameful ignorance, because you pretend that as far as they themselves are considered men fall and err by God's mere permission. This is an impious and sacrilegious invention, that God merely permits any evil for men with respect to themselves, when it is apparent that he severely prohibits and forbids whatever is contrary to his command. Nevertheless, why he allows men the choice to err, nay, even more by his secret decree he sentences men to error, men whom he commands to keep the way of his rule, cannot be comprehended by the sober and modest. To make inquiry in the shameless way that you do shows how brazen you are!

To suppose, as you do, that Christ was giving permission to his disciples to depart (John 6:67) shows how unskillful you are in interpreting this passage. Rather, by noting the defection of others he is exhorting his disciples to perseverance. When he sorrowfully asks them, "Do you want to go away as well?" he places a bridle upon them to prevent them disappearing along with the apostates. Does this way of speaking seem like permission to you? I acknowledge that common sense determines that to command is one thing and to permit is another. There is no dispute between us on that point, but our dispute is whether God passively watches what takes place on earth or whether he governs every single action of men with supreme authority. Or if the word gives you so much pleasure, you must make it clear whether the permission is willing or unwilling. This latter option is ruled out by what I read in the Psalms: "Our God is in the heavens; he does all that he pleases" (Ps. 115:3). But if it is a willing permission, it is an impious act for you to suppose that he is inactive. So it follows that by his counsel he governs whatever he wills to come to pass. It is extremely childish of you to weigh the sublime mysteries of God by the rules of common sense.

Now, let us consider your argument that Christ, who taught divine things, must accommodate them to common sense. It is clear that Christ himself boldly denies this and so proves that you are guilty of shameless lying. Do you not hear him when he teaches that he speaks in parables so that the common man hearing would not hear? (Matt. 13:13). It is certainly true that the Holy Spirit in a certain way speaks childishly, everywhere for our sakes imitating a nurse. Nevertheless, common sense is still greatly deficient to act as a substantial judge of his doctrine, which is too deep even for the capacities of angels. Paul declared, "The natural person does not accept the things of the Spirit of God" (1 Cor. 2:14).

Therefore he commands those who desire to make progress in the heavenly school to become fools and to empty themselves of their particular understanding. In short, God claims himself to be the universal enlightener of the mind.

There is not enough time and space to gather together all the testimonies from Scripture that condemn the common sense of the darkened mind. Therefore, if someone longs for the wisdom of God he must renounce his own wisdom and ask for heavenly light. One example will be sufficient. Because God did not will the doctrine of the gospel to be proclaimed to the Gentiles until the coming of Christ, Paul calls it a "mystery hidden for ages," unknown even to angels in heaven (Eph. 3:9). When you reckon that nothing is provable unless common sense is its judge and arbiter, you push common sense to the front in such a way that it overturns this doctrine whenever it wants to. Speaking of God's providence, the prophet exclaims, "How great are your works, O LORD! Your thoughts are very deep!" (Ps. 92:5). You, however, deny anything to be divine unless you are able to measure it with your very own reason. What is the meaning of Paul's admonition when he declares on the present subject, "But who are you, O man?" and "Oh, the depth of the riches and wisdom and knowledge of God! How unsearchable are his judgments and how inscrutable his ways!" (Rom. 9:20; 11:33). He commands us to marvel and to be astonished because when we come before the incomprehensible counsel of God all our understanding is deficient. But you will admit nothing unless you can see it for yourself.

Article 4: All the crimes that have been accomplished by any man are the good and just works of God.

You continue with your forgeries in the fourth article. My only desire is that the readers judge this article candidly on the basis of its own worth and not according to your foul objections. Not that I run to take refuge when you hurl these objections. I only complain that instead of my doctrine being faithfully presented, out of spiteful hatred you changed my words. And in a similar spirit you quarrel with me as if I said the just works of God are sin—a doctrine that I detest throughout my writings. Therefore, the more your arguments seem clever to you, the more your immaturity appears ridiculous. You infer that justice is evil and injustice is good, that God is the servant of sin, unjustly punishing his own work. All these monstrosities are fabrications of your own mind and have been diligently refuted by me, as my books testify. There is coming a time when you will certainly realize how detestable a crime it is to mock the hidden mysteries of God in a way that desecrates them.

Now let me show you that the business you dispute over is not with me but with the heavenly judge whose tribunal you will not escape. Job, by the inspiration of the Spirit, declares that what was done by Satan and by the robbers was the work of God (Job 1:21). At no point does he accuse God of sin, but blesses his holy name. When innocent Joseph was sold by his brothers, the act was an obvious atrocity. Yet when Joseph ascribes the same work to God, he dwells upon his immense goodness in providing food for his father's family (Gen. 45:5). When Isaiah declares Assyria to be the rod in the hand of God, he makes God to be the one through whom Assyria destroyed Israel with a horrible slaughter, without ascribing to God the least amount of stain (Isa. 10:5). Jeremiah curses those who negligently did the work of

God. When the prophet refers to the work of God, he means the cruelty perpetrated by the impious armies who were set against Israel (Jer. 48:10). Now, if you will, complain to him as if he had said that God had sinned. To sum up, all who are acquainted with Scripture are readily aware that so many instances of such testimonies could quickly be collected as to fill an entire volume. But why are words needed when the thing is evident to all?

Was it not a manifestation or proof of God's graciousness when he did not spare his own Son? Of Christ's as well because he delivered himself up? Here you are with an impure and sacrilegious mouth affirming that if the offering of his only begotten Son is the work of God, then God sinned. But all pious men, along with Augustine, easily untie this knot. "When the Father delivered up the Son, and the Lord gave up his own body, and Judas betrayed his Lord, why in this deliverance is God just and man guilty? Is it not because in the one thing that they did, the motives of God and man were not one and the same?"[27] Therefore, Peter does not hesitate plainly to assert that Pilate and the Jews, together with the rest of the ungodly, accomplished what the counsel and hand of God had decreed (Acts 4:28), just as shortly before he had declared that Christ was delivered up by the settled counsel and foreknowledge of God (Acts 2:23). If you decide to ignore the word *foreknowledge*, then the phrase "settled counsel" provides a convincing refutation of you. The first passage removes any ambiguity—Pilate and the ungodly did what the counsel and hand of God had decreed to be done.

---

[27]*Calvini Opera* has "Augustine, Letter 48 ad Vincentium." In the now-standard numbering of Augustine's letters, it is numbered 93. "Therefore, when the Father delivered up the Son, and Christ Himself delivered up Hs Body, and Judas delivered up His Master, why, in that delivering up, is God good and man guilty, except that though they all did the same thing, they did not do it for the same reason?' (*Letters 83–130*, trans. Wilfrid Parsons [Washington DC, The Catholic University of America Press, 1953], 63).

If you do not understand so great a secret, then at least refrain from offering thoughtless insults and instead marvel with the apostle and exclaim, "Oh, the depth!" If you would allow yourself to be teachable, then a fuller explanation is already provided for you from my other writings. On this occasion, so that the weak of mind will not be confused, it is enough for me simply to restrain your willfulness.

Article 5: No adultery, theft, or murder is committed without the will of God being involved. (Inst. 14.44.)

Article 6: Scripture clearly testifies that crimes are planned not only by the will of God but even by his authority.

It is through the providence of God, which you oppose, that you quote this passage in the fifth article. For our readers will see that in this passage I am reporting the objections against my own doctrine using the very words of my opponents in the way that they usually express themselves. Don't you deserve that all should spit in your face for grabbing hold of this mangled passage for your own purpose?[28]

In the sixth article, even though you do not provide a reference to the citation, your audacity nevertheless stands out by a mile. Whenever sin is mentioned in my writings I keep the name of God out of it, and this should be a serious warning to you. Wherever have I said that crimes are perpetrated not only by the will of God but also by his authority? I assure you that I am more than happy for such a terrible blasphemy to be utterly condemned. I ask only that you do not unjustly involve

---

[28]In the 1559 *Institutes* Battles translated the relevant passage (carried over from the 1539 and subsequent editions) as follows: "Does an assassin murder an upright citizen? He has carried out, they say, God's plan. Has someone stolen, or committed adultery? Because he has done what was foreseen and ordained by the Lord, he is the minister of God's providence. Has a son, neglecting remedies, with never a care awaited the death of a parent? He could not resist God, who had so appointed from eternity. Thus all crimes, because subject to God's ordinance, they call virtues" *Institutes* I.17.3.

my name with it. I am fully aware how successful you are in deceiving the foolish, but I am not afraid. If anyone takes the trouble to compare my writings with your inventions, they will come to detest you for your dishonesty, as you deserve to be.

You argue that if God loves sin, then he has a hatred for righteousness; and you add many similar thoughts. But why do you go to this trouble, unless it is to undermine my words? I first stated such things clearly enough not yesterday or the day before but many years ago. "If, in the robbing of Job, God, Satan, and the robbers acted together, how, if Satan and his instruments are guilty, can God be free from guilt? The answer is: if we distinguish one human action from another by means of their intention and end, then the cruelty of the one who digs out crows' eyes or kills the stork is condemned, while the sentence of the judge who deliberately commits himself to the execution of men is praised. So why should God be treated so shabbily that his justice is not made distinct from the crimes of men?"[29] Let readers merely skim through what I write there; on the contrary, let them read the entire work of the treatise where I engage in the defense of the providence of God. They will quickly discover that what is written there is more than sufficient to blow away all the smokescreens that you set up. Let them add to that, if they have a mind to, what I have written on the second chapter of Acts.[30]

When men commit the crimes of theft or murder, they sin

---

[29]Calvin appears to be quoting the following passage more or less verbatim. "We learn then that the work was jointly the work of God and of Satan and of the robbers. We learn that nothing happens but what seems good to God. How then is God to be exempted from the blame to which Satan with his instruments is liable? Of course a distinction is made between the deeds of men and their purpose and end; for the cruelty of the man who puts out the eyes of crows or kills a stork is condemned, while the virtue of the judge is praised who puts his hand to the killing of a criminal. Why should the case of God be worse so that we may not distinguish Him in His justice from the misdeeds of men?" (*Concerning the Eternal Predestination of God*, 180).
[30]Acts 2:20: "Here is a notable place touching the providence of God, that we may know that as well our life as our death is governed by it" *Commentary on the Acts of the Apostles*.

because they are thieves and murderers. At the root of their theft and murder is a wicked intention. God, who makes use of their malice, is a superior being in a loftier position. For inasmuch as he wills to chastise one person and to show patience to another, his intentions are altogether different. Therefore, he never deviates from his perfect uprightness. Because a wicked action is to be judged by the end toward which it is directed, it is quite clear that God is not the author of sin. The sum of the matter is this: since the cause of evil lies in the evil will of men, God exercises his right judgments by their hands in such a way that he is utterly blameless, and in an utterly marvelous way he brings the light of his glory out of the darkness of sin.

Also in that tract, which stirred up against me these furies from the deepest hell, the following clear distinction occurs. Nothing is more wicked or more preposterous than to drag God into fellowship with guilt when he executes his judgments through the hands of the Devil and the impious, since there is no affinity in their reasons for acting.[31] A work was published by me twelve years ago that is more than sufficient to vindicate me from your foul objections.[32] If there had been one drop of humanity in you and those like you, then this ought to have provided immunity to me from all this trouble. I will not now boast about the skill by which I refute the madness by which the Libertines entice so many. Most certainly I have with set purpose taken up the cause of God and demonstrated with utter clarity that God is not the author of sin.

---

[31]See, e.g., *Concerning the Eternal Predestination of God*, 162ff.

[32]This is presumably a reference to Calvin's writing against the Libertines, published in 1545, translated by B. W. Farley as *Against the Fantastic and Furious Sect of the Libertines Who Are Called "Spirituals"* in *Treatises Against the Anabaptists and Against the Libertines* (Grand Rapids: Baker, 1982). In chap. 14, Calvin discusses divine providence in the light of the pantheism of the Libertines that obliterates the distinction between primary and second causes. "Satan and evildoers are not so effectively the instruments of God that they do not also act in their own behalf" (245).

Article 7: Whatever men bring about when they sin, they do so by the will of God, so much so that the will of God often clashes with his precepts.

I am not at all interested in responding to this seventh article. You must first produce the passage where I declare that the will of God is often opposed to his precept, for such a thing has never come into my mind. I have not even dreamt it. Rather the contrary. I faithfully expounded how the will of God is one and simple, although some discrepancy may appear between his secret counsel and what he requires of us. Whoever submits to the will of God modestly and soberly, insofar as he appreciates the smallness of the human intellect, will easily understand how God, who forbids whoredom and yet punishes the adultery of David through the incest of Absalom, always wills one thing, though in different ways. Therefore, in order that your false accusations do not cast a stain on me, this is a brief account of my position for the reader. Though you spread the idea that I teach two contrary wills in God, this is a wicked lie which you have made up, since it is everywhere preached by me that there is perfect agreement between God's secret counsel and the expression of his external command.

I recognize that Augustine conceded that God has two different wills, but these are in such agreement with one another that it will be made clear in the last days that there is little or no difference in his complex ways of reasoning.[33] This being established, now fight with yourself if you want to, "if God forbids what he wills to be done or commands what he does not will, he commands that his will is to be resisted." Nothing in this filth is recognizable as my teaching.

On the contrary, this is the sum of my doctrine: that which

---

[33]This is a possible reference to two wills in Augustine, e.g., *Enchiridion*, 100.

is expressed in the law is the will of God, so that it is clearly demonstrated that he approves uprightness and hates iniquity. It is certain that, if it pleased him, he would not prevent the punishment of the wicked. However, nothing hinders God, by his ineffable counsel, from causing something that he does not will and forbids to be done, to be done for a different end. If you here oppose me by claiming that God contradicts himself,[34] I would ask in return: is it for you to judge God's ability and to prescribe to him your own law? Moses teaches, "The secret things belong to the LORD our God, but the things that are revealed belong to us and to our children forever, that we may do all the words of this law" (Deut. 29:29).

Are you prepared to believe that nothing is lawful for God that you do not fully understand? In the book of Job, after the depth of God's counsel that overwhelms all human understanding is celebrated, finally this clause is added: "Behold, these are but the outskirts of his ways, and how small a whisper do we hear of him! But the thunder of his power who can understand?" (Job 26:14). But you will not allow that God has a single intention that you do not immediately recognize. So, either you are completely blind, or you recognize that when God speaks and forbids adultery, it follows that he is not willing that you should be an adulterer. And yet in the adulteries that he condemns, he exercises just judgment, and he could not do this unless he does so knowingly and willingly.

This can be stated more briefly, if you wish—he wills that adultery should not be committed in so far as it is a pollution, a violation of the sacred order, and a transgression of his law. To whatever extent he utilizes these adulteries and other wickedness for the execution of his vengeance, he certainly

---

[34] Lit. "fights his own tail."

does not discharge his office of judge unwillingly. The cruelty of the Assyrians and the Chaldeans as they were carrying out a horrible slaughter is most certainly not to be praised. On the contrary, God himself announces that he will be vindicated against them, yet he again makes known that in this way sacrifices were prepared for him.[35] Will you deny God the right to will that which dignifies his honorable name by sacrifice? So rouse yourself at last and acknowledge that when men are driven headfirst by a depraved appetite, God in his secret and ineffable way accomplishes his judgments.

You think that your deception is subtle when you ask, "From the command of God forbidding adultery, does he will all to be adulterers or only a part?" For if I respond "in part," you infer that God is inconsistent with himself. Now, you yourself have a confident answer, namely that God demands that all men be chaste because he loves all men. Yet even if I were silent, experience itself reveals that there are different reasons for his willing. For if his will were equally efficacious that all men be chaste, then without doubt he would bring it about that all were chaste. Since chastity is his unique gift, experience shows that in what he commands in his Word he wills differently from what he brings to pass by the Spirit of regeneration. So there is no reason why you, with your shameless tongue, should reproach God for hypocrisy, as if he had both honey and venom in his mouth. For when he commands or forbids, God does not pretend, but his nature is sincerely disclosed. In his secret will, by which he directs the actions of men, you will find nothing contrary to his justice.

---

[35]Calvin's thought is that the punishments of the opponents of God's people were to be understood as sacrificial offerings to his glory. See, e.g., his commentary on Isa. 34:6: "He compares it to *sacrifices*, for animals are slain in sacrifice for the worship and honor of God, and in like manner the destruction of this people will also tend to the glory of God." See also Jer. 46:10 and Ezek. 39:17.

Whoredom displeases God, who is the author of purity, yet God wills to punish David with the lustful incest of Absalom. He forbids the shedding of human blood as he pursues his image that he loves and watches over him with his protection. And yet out of the impious nations he raised up executioners for the sons of Eli because he willed to kill them.[36] This is what sacred history teaches us. If your blindness hinders you, yet all who have eyes see that God is consistent when he hates whoredom and slaughter insofar as they are sins and abhors the transgression of his law in whoredom and slaughter, and yet through the same whoredom and wickedness of every kind, he executes his judgments by justly punishing the sins of men.

However skillful your questions may appear to you, "If there is any secret will of God, how was it made available to me?" I have no difficulty in responding to it, so long as you permit me to follow my master, the Holy Spirit. For if God, as Paul testifies, "dwells in unapproachable light" (1 Tim. 6:16), if the same apostle with good reason exclaims that his ways are inscrutable (Rom. 11:33), why am I not allowed to marvel at his secret will even though it is concealed from us? In the book of Job there are many splendid eulogies that celebrate the wisdom of God so that mere mortals may learn not to measure God's wisdom by their own understanding. Will you then ridicule all that discussion concerning about what is secret? Will you reproach David for the same foolish reports about God's judgments, when he acknowledged them to be a deep abyss? (Ps. 36:7). From every prophet and apostle I hear the same thing: that the counsel of God is incomprehensible. I embrace by faith without reserve what they declare and what

---

[36] 1 Samuel 3–4.

I believe I freely and confidently declare. Why should such modesty be reckoned to me as a fault?

You cannot turn your back on the challenge by saying that I have used examples that are irrelevant to the case in hand. For I certainly share the same cause with Paul when he exclaims, regarding the deep wisdom that God displays in secret election or reprobation, "How unsearchable are his judgments and how inscrutable his ways!"[37] For all this he does not cease to assert publicly that God shows mercy to whom he wills, while the others he sentences to destruction. In conclusion, you must move beyond this childish dilemma that pleases you so much, for Scripture furnishes me with a testimony of God's secret will. What I have learned to grasp from Scripture, I speak with certainty. Since I do not reach for the heights, I reverently adore with humility and trepidation what is too sublime even for angels. Therefore, I often advise in my writings that there is nothing greater than to possess a wise ignorance, for those who engage in attempting to know more than they should rave like madmen.

You now see how certain I am about that will of God to which the Scriptures testify. The will of God remains secret in that even the minds of angels cannot fully grasp why God wills something to be, or how he wills it to be. Your pride deludes you and those like you to such an extent that whatever escapes or surpasses your understanding you try to make vanish into nothingness.

In my view your objections about the existence of contradictions are now more than satisfied and are of no further concern. Nevertheless, you attack me with a humor that is offensive as well as foolish, and that is insulting to me. If I

---

[37]Rom. 11:33.

am an imitator of God as you claim, then you deny that any faith can have a double tongue, a double heart, or a double will. By-and-by you will know what it means to imitate the Devil by ascending to the highest that you might be exalted like him. What torment me the most are your rabid blasphemies by which you spit against the sacred majesty of God, of which he himself will be the vindicator. As the will of God is good, which he has revealed in the law, I concede that whatever is contrary to it is evil. But you are babbling about the alleged contradictions in the secret will of God by which he distinguishes the vessels of mercy from the vessels of wrath, and through which, for his own purposes, he freely makes use of both. From the stinking pit of your own ignorance you breathe out a fabrication that is as detestable as it is false.

I confess that Christ speaks of his public will when he says, "O Jerusalem, Jerusalem, the city that kills the prophets and stones those who are sent to it! How often would I have gathered your children together as a hen gathers her brood under her wings, and you would not!" (Luke 13:34). He reproaches the Jews in the same way that Moses does in his song (Deut. 32:11). And we know that God certainly fulfills what these words express. The doctrine of the law and the exercises of piety and the great kindness by which God binds his people to himself were nothing other than God expanding his wings to protect them, if their untamed wildness had not dragged them off somewhere else. When, therefore, Christ attempted so many times and in so many different ways through his prophets to call back those perverse nations to his discipline, he reasonably complains of their ingratitude. By restricting your comments to the life of Christ, you disclose your customary ignorance; as if he were not the true God, who from the beginning has not ceased to spread forth his wings of grace. Then you infer that if he had another contrary will, then his whole life would be hypocrisy. As if to allure by voice and by offering benefits yet not to influence the heart by the secret inspiration of the Spirit is to act in a truly contrary fashion.

To make the futility of this objection more obvious, when he complains at having been disappointed because the vine he expected to bring forth sweet fruit produced sour wine (Isa. 5:4), what do you, the great rhetorician, make of this? To avoid making it seem as if he was deceived, are you going to reckon him to be ignorant of the future? According to you, the Jews were frustrating the purposes of God; the outcome was doubtful to him because he was uncertain about the future. As if a certain manner of speaking, which refers only to the event considered in itself, ought to be applied to the secret foreknowledge of God.

Elsewhere he says, "Surely you will fear me," yet they with eagerness to corrupt themselves increased more and more (Zeph. 3:7). God promises himself some fruit to proceed from the punishments inflicted, and yet afterwards he complains of being deceived. Can you set yourself free from this position only by making God to depend upon the free will of man, which in this way confines him? As if it were not sufficiently clear, he magnifies the crimes of man by dressing himself in the character of a person who says, when the outcome is a failure, that his labor is for nothing. Whoever God efficaciously wills to gather to himself, he draws by his Spirit, and, because this is in his hands, he promises that he will do it. Therefore, as many as are called and do not follow, it is more than certain that the mode of gathering that Christ mourns as fruitless and vain must differ from the efficacious call that he mentions elsewhere. See, for example, where Isaiah says, "He will gather the dispersed of Judah" (Isa. 11:12), "the glory of the Lord will gather you" (Isa. 58:8), from the west I will gather you" (Isa. 43:5), and "your God will gather you" (Isa. 52:12).[38] This is because God had previously laid bare his arm so that his mighty works might be made visible in the sight of the nations. Therefore, a little after he repeats, "For a brief moment I deserted you, but with great compassion I will gather you" (Isa. 54:7).

What I have said concerning the precepts of God is more than sufficient to quench your blasphemies, for God gives no insincere precepts but seriously reveals what he wills and commands. However, while in one way he wills that his elect fulfill his obedience by efficaciously persuading them, in another way he warns the reprobate by means of an external word but does not consider them worthy to draw them to himself. Stubbornness and depravity are equally natural to all men, so that none are of themselves willing and able to take up the yoke. To some, God promises the Spirit of obedience, but others remain in their depravity. For whatever you might babble to the contrary, the new, living heart is not promised to all indiscriminately but peculiarly to the elect so that they might walk in God's precepts. What can you say to this, good judge? When God invites the whole crowd to himself, and yet the Spirit was knowingly and willingly held back from the greater part, nevertheless he draws a few by his secret inspiration to obedience. Is this to be condemned as a lie?

---

[38]What Calvin translates as "gather you" in Isa. 58:2 and 52:12 the ESV, e.g., has "be your rearguard."

Article 8: The hardening of Pharaoh, indeed even his stubbornness of soul and rebellion, was the work of God. Moses testifies to this, according to whom the whole rebellion of Pharaoh is to be attributed to the will of God.

Article 9: The will of God is the supreme cause of the hardness of men's hearts.

Here again I implore the reader honestly to compare my words and all my teaching with your mutilated articles. Then, when your objections, by which you work so hard to arouse hatred, are seen for what they really are, they will lose all credibility and vanish into thin air. Meanwhile, I do not deny having declared, with both Moses and Paul, that the heart of Pharaoh was hardened by God. Here, showing contempt for Moses, as if you have no regard for his word, you demand from me an answer to this question: "When the same Moses said, 'Pharaoh hardened his own heart,' why do you strive for the harsher interpretation, "God hardened Pharaoh's heart"?

I do not need to ask for a solution to this from any other source other than from the words of the ninth article, where your quotation is either distorted or misunderstood. For if, when a man hardens his own heart, then the will of God is the preeminent or the remote cause of the hardening, and he himself is the more immediate cause. I distinguish everywhere between primary and secondary causes and between mediate and proximate causes. While the sinner discovers in himself the root cause of his evil affections, he is certain not to credit God with his guilt. Somewhere I have said that to do this is to be just like the nurse of Medea, the ancient poet, who said, "If only the pine trees of the earth had not been chopped down with axes in the forest of Pelion." Now, when that impure woman felt herself being driven by her own lust to betray her father's kingdom, this foolish nurse blames neither her own shameless affections nor the enticement of Jason,[39] but complains instead that a ship has been built in Greece! When a man who is conscious of his own wickedness invokes remote causes as a pretext for dismissing from his mind his own guilt, he shows that he is ridiculously unaware of himself.

So you now see that although God hardens a man's heart in his own way, nevertheless the man's hardness is justly imputed to him, because everyone is hardened by his own wickedness. It is an altogether different matter when hearts are being bent toward God in obedience to him; for all are by nature predisposed toward disobedience. No one desires to conduct himself rightly unless he is in fact acted upon by God. Yet were Scripture to declare both that hearts are prepared by God and that the faithful prepare themselves to present willing worship to God, it would contradict itself. Instead, Scripture distinctly discloses that the true worshipers of God, spontaneously and willingly by the affections of their hearts, do what they ought to do, and also that God fulfills his part by the secret stirring of the Spirit. It is altogether different as far as hardening is concerned, just as I have already said, because God does not govern reprobates by the Spirit of regeneration but surrenders and gives them over to the Devil. He also governs their depraved affections by his secret judgment so

---

[39]Calvin had previously used this illustration in *Concerning the Eternal Predestination of God*, 8.5, 122. The line that Calvin quotes is from the start of Euripides' *Medea*:
"SCENE: Before Medea's house in Corinth, near the palace of Creon. The Nurse enters from the house.
NURSE: Ah! Would to Heaven the good ship Argo ne'er had sped its course to the Colchian land through the misty blue Symplegades, nor ever in the glens of Pelion the pine been felled to furnish with oars the chieftain's hands, who went to fetch the golden fleece for Pelias; for then would my own mistress Medea never have sailed to the turrets of Iolcos, her soul with love for Jason smitten, nor would she have beguiled the daughters of Pelias to slay their father and come to live here in the land of Corinth with her husband and children, where her exile found favour with the citizens to whose land she had come, and in all things of her own accord was she at one with Jason, the greatest safeguard this when wife and husband do agree; but now their love is all turned to hate, and tenderest ties are weak" (http://classics.mit.edu/Euripides/medea.html, lines 1–10).

that nothing is done unless he decrees it. These things agree harmoniously with one another—that in whatever manner God hardens whom he wills, each person is still the author of his own hardening.

So that I might not be tedious, the readers might be helped by this fine admonition by Augustine: "Whereas the apostle declares that men are handed over to perverse affections, this is wrongfully and ignorantly restricted to suffering, because Paul elsewhere connects power with suffering. He said, 'What if God, desiring to show his wrath and to make known his power, has endured with much patience vessels of wrath prepared for destruction?' (Rom. 9:22)."[40] And although that holy teacher never wrote on this subject, the authority of God alone ought to be more than satisfying. I did not state that God withdrew understanding from the princes of this world so that he might cause them to err or that he mastered the heart of Pharaoh so that he might not turn toward humanity. Nor did I say that God turned the hearts of the nations or strengthened them in hatred toward his people when hissing for the Egyptians, to use them as hammers. I did not say that Sennacherib was a rod in the hand of God, but the Spirit pronounces it. What? When Scripture also says that Saul was seized by an evil spirit from God, will you attribute this only to allowance and permission (1 Sam. 18:10)? How much more accurate is the admonishment of Augustine (in his book on holy predestination): "If Satan and the impious sin, it is of themselves; if they do this

---

[40]*C. Jul.* 5.3.13: What do you mean when you say, 'When they are said to have been handed over to their desires, they should be understood to have been abandoned to sins by God's patience, not forced to them by his power'? You say this as if the same apostle did not mention these both at once when he said, 'What if God, desiring to show his wrath and to make known his power, has endured with much patience vessels of wrath prepared for destruction' (Romans 9.22)" (*Answer to the Pelagians* 2, The Works of St. Augustine: A Translation for the 21st Century, introduction, trans., and notes Roland J. Teske [Hyde Park, NY: New City Press, 1998], 441).

or that when sinning, it is by the power of God who divides the darkness as it pleases him."[41]

You credit to me whatever God openly declares. Allow the same Augustine to respond to you for me: "Scripture, if diligently studied, reveals that he directs not only the good wills of men, which he fashions from evil to good works and eternal life, but that those wills which most certainly retain their worldly nature are also in the power of God so that he is able to incline them as he pleases when he pleases, either to confer blessing or to inflict punishment by his secret, but just, judgment."[42]

Article 10: Satan is a liar by the command of God.

In the tenth article, look against whom you are throwing poisonous darts. You do not oppose what is particular to me but what proceeds from the Spirit of God. Thus Scripture speaks explicitly, "Who will I send? Who will go up for us?" Immediately afterward calling upon Satan, he commands him to go that he might be a lying spirit in the mouth of all the prophets for the purpose of deceiving Ahab (1 Kings 22:20–23). You may bark as much as you please. You will no more bury the glory of God with your insults than you will darken the radiance of the sun with spittle. Here also the words of Augustine surpass what I have to say: "When God testifies to have sent false prophets himself, and that his hand is upon

---

[41] This appears to be a paraphrase of the following passage: "It is, then, in the power of the evil to sin, but it is not in their power, but in the power of God, who divides the darkness and orders it to his ends that, by sinning in their malice, they bring about this or that effect" ("The Predestination of the Saints," in *Answer to the Pelagians 4*, trans. Teske, Works of St. Augustine, 176).

[42] "If the divine scripture is examined with care, it shows that not only the good wills which God himself produces out of evil ones and which, once made good by him, he directs toward good acts and toward eternal life, but also those wills which preserve the creature of the world are in the power of God so that he makes them turn where he wills and when he wills, either to offer benefits to some or to impose punishments on others, as he himself judges by his judgment which is, of course, most hidden, but undoubtedly most just ("Grace and Free Choice," in *Answer to the Pelagians 4*, trans. Teske, Works of St. Augustine, 99).

them so that they may deceive, this does not refer only to his patience, but also to his power."[43]

As regards the next point, in so far as you blabber about Satan not being obedient when he lies by the command of God, it is no wonder that you entangle yourself in many knots. You do not acknowledge that God employs the work of Satan according to his judgment so that he might display the justice and righteousness of his command and not free from guilt the servant whom he compels to carry out his judgment unwillingly. Even if your bitterness should resound a hundred times over, this is certainly not the voice of Calvin but of God: "I have commanded my holy ones" (Isa. 13:3). Now, if you think that God has taken more than is proper to himself, he will absolve himself of your accusations.

Article 11: God grants the will to perform evil. Furthermore, he prompts perverse and dishonest affections, not just permissively but effectually, in order to further his own glory.

You proceed to invent monsters so that by defeating them you might celebrate a triumph over an inoffensive servant of God. You will never discover anywhere that I might have said these things. In any case, even if I remain silent, uniting foolishness with impudence (as you do) has ruined your case. I teach that if the impious contaminate themselves with slaughter, adultery, rape, and fraud, it is from their own wickedness. Yet God, who draws light out of darkness, rules within them by his own secret and incomprehensible judgment so that he might accomplish his just judgments through their wickedness. If you oppose this, you contend with God himself, who will easily ward off your mad accusations. This distinction that

---

[43]This direct quotation seems in fact to be a paraphrase or free rendering of part of Augustine's argument in *Against Julian*, 5.3.

constantly occurs in my writings would undoubtedly satisfy you if you possessed but one drop of modesty or gentleness.

If the wicked examine themselves, the testimony of consciousness abundantly convicts them that they need not search for the fault anywhere else, because they have discovered the root of wickedness within their heart. Yet God used their wickedness for good by bending their depraved wills however it pleased him. However much you murmur in protest, I have time and again shown that you seek a quarrel not with me but with God. If only you would from your heart acknowledge God to be the Father of lights, as the apostle Paul defines him (1 Tim. 6:16). Then in your audacity you would not try to break through to the light inaccessible. No; even more so, you would not turn that light into darkness by your sacrilegious impudence.

Moreover, from the doctrine of James you foolishly infer that because every perfect gift descends from the Father of lights, the horrible judgments that lead the pious to become frightened and tremble do not descend from the same source (James 1:17). You still foolishly ask me if I count vicious and perverse affections along with good gifts, as if the spirit of wisdom, justice, and prudence did not truly differ from the spirit of giddiness or as if the Spirit of regeneration that renews the faithful in the image of God was no other than an evil spirit of God that, as we read of Saul, hurls the reprobate into madness. With the same impudence you also attack what I teach about God exercising his own judgments for his glory through the work of Satan and the reprobate. God clearly testifies by his Word and through experience that Satan is the instrument of his wrath.

Now, for what purpose, if not to magnify his own glory,

will we say that God worked through the hand of Satan? You think you can escape this question with witty jokes, saying that righteousness is not attributed to God from deception, but will you hinder God from bringing forth material from your wickedness for his own glory? Certainly Pharaoh was only able to prevent the divine glory from shining forth by nothing less than his immense pride because he had been ordained for this purpose. You plead that Nebuchadnezzar gave glory to God when he confessed his justice (Dan. 4:34–37). So that you may know that I confidently disregard your blunted darts, I willingly help you in this case and will furnish you with what did not come to your mind. When Joshua exhorted Achan to give glory to God, it was for no other end except that he might reveal his own sacrilege by exposing the lie of Achan (Josh. 7:19).

But now this is the question at hand: is there only one way that the glory of God can be manifested? Because if it does not shine forth from the lies of men, then Paul was deceived when he said, "Let God be true, though every one were a liar" and immediately afterward asks, "If our unrighteousness serves to show the righteousness of God, what shall we say? That God is unrighteous to inflict wrath on us?" (Rom. 3:4–5).[44] Because you object that God should be praised for his benefits, it is indeed true only if you concede that the ways[45] by which God advances and draws up his praise is manifold. Here your pride is justly punished because you profess to mock the art of reasoning and always to argue negatively from species to genus.[46] Nor will I dignify your slanderous joke by replying to

---

[44]"to inflict wrath upon us" is not in Calvin's original text, but it is the Romans text.
[45]Calvin has "sylvam" here, which can be literally translated as "masses."
[46]That is, Calvin is saying that Castellio makes the logical mistake of claiming that because God should be praised for one kind of benefit, therefore all praiseworthy benefits from God must be of this same kind.

it, where you argue that God is unjust if he punishes men for having a beard inasmuch as they wear a beard because this is how he created them.

Whoever has said that iniquity was created by God, even though in his incomprehensible counsel he ordains it for just and right ends? Therefore, be gone with your stupidity where you compare a beard that grows naturally in sleep with voluntary wickedness. However long you continue in your madness, this will remain fixed with us—that the perverse instruments that God determines and rules for the purpose of executing his just judgments are rightly punished because of their own awareness of acting wickedly.

Now see how you get yourself into a tangle while confessing that God's secrets are unknown to us. You claim the contrary, that God's justice is not known by us. If anyone were to ask you, "Is there any justice in God's secrets or is there not?" will you truly deny it? Again, will you say his justice is not known to us, when David and Paul admire it with wonder because their understanding fails them? Do the great depth and the rich loftiness of wisdom in the judgments of God not contain justice? Why will you, therefore, deny that God is just whenever the reason for his work is hidden from you?

In the book of Job a noteworthy distinction is established between the unsearchable wisdom of God, which the human race is denied access to, and the wisdom that is delivered to us in the law (Job 28:27). Thus, unless you confound everything, you also ought to have distinguished between the profound and admirable justice that cannot be captured by the human mind and the rule of justice that is prescribed in the law for regulating the life of man. I acknowledge that God will judge the world according to the revealed doctrine of the gospel, but he will also vindicate the equity of his secret providence against all adversaries.

Now, if you were in the least skilled in the gospel that you speak foolishly against, you would easily understand how God rewards the justice that he commands in his law and never deprives the promised crown to those who wholeheartedly obey his precepts. Yet he punishes all the immoral that he calls his servants because he has their hearts in his hands. Nebuchadnezzar, who was a mad plunderer and a slave to Satan, is in the writings of Jeremiah with good reason called a servant of God (Jer. 25:9). I have said that God is able to open a way for his judgment by inspiring the hearts of men for this or that. Why, when prophets have said the same things in so many words, is this accredited to me as a crime? These are truly the words of sacred history: "Again the anger of the LORD was kindled against Israel, and he incited David against them, saying, 'Go number Israel and Judah'" (2 Sam. 24:1).

Article 12: The impious, in their impiety, produce more of God's work than their own.

Again, such things have never been said by me. I testify in the presence of God, the angels, and the whole world that that which is truly spoken by me is wickedly and calumniously perverted by you. If it seems absurd to you that the wicked accomplish the work of God, then scold Jeremiah whose words these are: "Cursed is he who does the work of the LORD with slackness, and cursed is he who keeps back his sword from bloodshed" (Jer. 48:10). He refers to a murder that you will not absolve of criminality because it is evident that it is accomplished by their greed, cruelty, and pride. The Chaldeans were impelled by their own ambition and their lust for plunder so that they might inhumanly go step-by-step through rape and slaughter, unmindful of any sense of equity. But as it was pleasing to God to punish the Moabites by their hands, their depravity did not hinder God from executing his judgment. This is what you bark at, you dog, that impiety is good, as if the work of God is impious when he marvelously accommodates the wickedness of man for a different end than they intended. Indeed, you do not hesitate to throw me among the Libertines, a sect whose madness I have exposed before all and refuted, so that I do not need to look for a new defense.

Article 13: From the perspective of God we sin necessarily, whether we sin on account of our own purpose or by accident.

Article 14: Whatever perversions men perpetrate by their own will, those also proceed from the will of God.

I can only understand what you intend in the last article if it is your practice to strike human understanding dumb by engaging in magical whispers. For what is it to sin by chance? And who except yourself has invented such a monster? I have said somewhere that the things which appear to have happened by chance are governed by the secret providence of God.[47] Who will therefore permit you to conclude that sin is fortuitous? As far as what is found in my writings, does it originate from me, or does it not rather have God as its author? If the hatchet that chops down the branches of a tree falls and wounds the head of a traveler, do you conclude that happens by chance? But the Holy Spirit, through Moses, declares that this man was killed by God. [48] Will you say that God blindly rains down his blows, right and left, like a drunk?

If you imagine that men sin without the knowledge of God,

---

[47]E.g., *Institutes*, 1539, incorporated into *Institutes* I.16.8 (1559).
[48]A possible allusion to Deut. 19:5.

how will God judge the world? And if the affairs in the world avoid his notice, how does he surpass mere mortals? When I declare that God brings to pass the sins of men, you are carried away in your madness so that you accuse me of creating a false god. If I were to concede what is demanded by you, that God is ignorant of sin, I ask you, what kind of a God would he be? And will you boast that the people are with you when you deprive God of understanding and dignify him with the same title that Lucretius gave to his images, so that you fabricate a dead idol in his place?[49] You argue, "If men sin necessarily, then teaching is superfluous, precepts useless, admonitions vain, correction and threats absurd." If Augustine's book to Valentinus, *Concerning Corruption and Grace* (a work dedicated to this very subject),[50] is not sufficient to dissolve this objection, you are not worthy to hear a word from me. Still, I have refuted Pighius[51] and your master Servetus[52] concerning this objection, so that as far as skilled and candid readers are concerned, nothing very great is required of me.

So now I will respond only briefly to your boastful objection. If you will not permit God to command that which is beyond human faculties, when you stand at his tribunal God will make it plain that he asserted nothing from the mouth of his apostle that was spoken in vain, "for God has done what the law, weakened by the flesh, could not do" (Rom. 8:3). A perfect justice is certainly revealed in the law that is available and made evident for all, if only our strength were sufficient

---

[49]A reference to the Epicurean Lucretius (c.99–c.55 BC) who, in his *De Rerum Natura (On the Nature of Things)*, claimed that physical objects produce "idols" (or images) of themselves that affect our senses and provide the basis of our knowledge of the material world.

[50]Translated with the title "On Rebuke and Grace," in *Answer to the Pelagians 4*, trans. Teske, Works of St. Augustine.

[51]In *Concerning the Eternal Predestination of God*, the second of his writings against Pighius and others, Calvin addresses the objection that "teaching is vain and exhortations empty and useless, if the strength and power to obey depend on the election of God," 135.

[52]It is not clear which of his writings Calvin is referring to.

to fulfill what God commands. And Paul declares that it is impossible to acquire righteousness from the law. Therefore, what is your dispute with Calvin? If you steal of necessity, do you suppose that you are no less excusable after the precept than before? Paul, on the contrary, when he confesses that he was sold under sin (Rom. 7:14), freely exclaims at the same time that the law works wrath (Rom. 4:15), so that the shield of necessity is in vain pleaded as an excuse when every man is convicted by his awareness of his own voluntary wickedness. I ask you, when last year the hook was in your hand for the purpose of stealing firewood so that you might warm your home, was it not your own will that drove you to steal? If this alone does not suffice for your just condemnation, that knowingly and willingly you disgracefully and wickedly gained at the expense of another, whatever you roar against necessity, this does not in the least secure your acquittal.

Now, concerning your objection that no one is justly condemned unless it is on account of a crime and after a crime, I have no quarrel with you on the former point, since I teach everywhere that no one dies except by the just judgment of God. At the same time, it is not lawful to conceal the secret venom that lurks in your words. For if the similarity that you propose is allowed, God is unjust when he involves the entire race of Abraham in the guilt of original sin. You deny God the liberty to condemn any mortal unless it is for actual sin. An innumerable number of infants are being taken away even today. Now declare (if you dare) your virulence against God because he casts down innocent babes from their mothers' breast into eternal death. When this blasphemy is clearly seen and the person does not repudiate it, they may curse me as much as they please, for it is not for me to demand immunity for myself from those who do not even spare God himself from the very same abuse.

In the second section,[53] consider how uncouth your loquacity is. Even your masters Servetus and Pighius and dogs like them would at least say that those whom God foreknew to be worthy of death were condemned before the creation of the world. In truth you will not permit him to sentence anyone to eternal death unless he is declared guilty by earthly judges for the actual perpetration of a crime. Hence, let the reader conclude how prodigious is your madness by which you do not hesitate to overthrow the entire order of divine justice.[54]

It now remains only for me to vindicate the glory of the true and eternal God from such sacrilegious insults. You hurl the accusation against me of promoting the Devil into the place of God. My defense is brief and easy. As all my writings clearly testify, I have no other concern than that the world should devote itself to God in a pious and holy way, and that everyone should cultivate sincere righteousness with each other with a pure conscience. My life is not inconsistent with my doctrine. I will not be unjust to the grace of God and so compare myself with you and those like you, whose innocence is nothing other than self-flattery. I will only say this, that if any upright and righteous judge should decide between us, he would recognize a clear reverence for God in my writing and in my life and that the only thing that you express is a spirit which mocks true piety.

Now that I might briefly strike down your objections, is it possible to imagine anything more profane than when you contend that God is slow to mercy and quick to wrath because

---

[53]This appears to be a reference to the last sentences of Castellio's comments on article fourteen, in which he rules out any doctrine of eternal reprobation.

[54]Calvin has no break here, but it seems that at this point he changes to the false God charges.

he determined the larger part of the world to eternal death? It is certain that whatever kind of god you have fabricated, it is the true God alone who is to be worshiped by all the pious. This is the same God who for more than 2,500 years allowed the human race, except the one race of Abraham, to wander in a deadly darkness. If you accuse him of cruelty because he willed that one family was set forth as the exception, being blessed with the light of life, while he willed to hurl innumerable families in death, the defense is evident. The nations were not destroyed daily and the whole world was not swallowed up one hundred times a year. In this way God gave illustrious proof of his patience. Truly Paul does not hesitate to praise his leniency and long-suffering when he asserts that the vessels of wrath are prepared for destruction by his secret decree (Rom. 9:12).

If you are not content with this testimony, I think it is surely lawful for me to despise your barking. God does not require any protection from me, because he is sufficiently qualified and able to be the defender of his justice, even if every impure tongue conspires to darken his name out of rivalry against him. You and your followers may hurl your blasphemies as high in the air as you please, but they will fall back on your own heads. It is not irksome for me to receive your insults patiently, so long as they do not reach the God whom I serve. I must also be permitted to call you forth to his tribunal, where he will appear in his own time to vindicate his doctrine that you madly oppose in my person.

Readers will judge how appropriate your account of God's true nature is when they recognize that your starting point is common sense. The existence of God is received with favor by all nations and ages since the principle and seed of this knowledge was implanted naturally in the mind of man. How will reason define what kind of God this is when, with her keen vision, she is able to do nothing except turn the truth into a lie and to provide reasons to adulterate the light and understanding of true faith and religion? The Holy Spirit commands us to become fools so that we might become disciples of heavenly doctrine, since the natural man is not able to grasp or experience it (1 Cor. 2:14). You, however, would have the mysteries of God judged by the power of human understanding and promote the reason that completely extinguishes the glory of God to the position of guide and instructor. This is not to mention that you act too boldly in preferring reason to Scripture.

Now it is no wonder that you permit the most opposite of religions to be indiscriminately confounded, so that you consider the Turk who worships an unknown god ignorantly, being dyed with the madness of Mohammed, to be a worshiper of God, equal with the Christian who has an unwavering faith in the gospel and calls upon the Father of our Redeemer. Though you do not earnestly protect the infidels publicly, the great amount of indirect mockery that you make clearly manifests that your purpose is to tear down the principles of our faith. It is also your practice to overthrow what the sacred oracles of the true God teach, by pleading as an excuse the superstitions of the nations. That very reason, which is the mother of all errors, has brought forth this God of yours who wills that everyone will be saved without distinction. As if the word *election*, which occurs so many times in Scripture, was truly an empty concept, when the law, the prophets, and the gospel everywhere proclaim that to be called and enlightened to salvation is to be elected by the eternal decree of God before the foundation of the world.

Also they declare without any question that the source and cause of life is the free love of God that does not lay hold of all but only those whom he wills. What do you accomplish by roaring against this one hundred times over? You blind the eyes of the simple by throwing up the smokescreen that God wills all to be saved. If this is incompatible with that election by which he predestined his children to life, then I ask you, why is the way of salvation not made available to all? That inscription of the law is well known and honored: "See, I have set before you today life and good, death and evil" (Deut. 30:15). If God willed to gather everyone to salvation without discrimination, why does he not propose life to all in common instead of distinguishing only one nation by this prerogative? If we believe Moses, this is for no other reason than that he freely loves those whom he elects for his own possession.

You say that Christ was sent by God so that his righteousness might superabound wherever sin abounded, but this one expression proves that you came forth from hell by the inspiration of the Devil. You audaciously ridicule Christ by covering up the crassness of your deceit with the colors of piety. If the righteousness of Christ superabounds wherever sin reigns, the condition of Pilate or Judas is no worse than that of Peter or Paul. And even were I to be silent about Pilate, Paul denies the possibility of separating the righteousness of Christ from the faith of the gospel. Will you tell us what gospel was in France and other foreign nations at the time when Christ lived on this earth? What? Was God not the same before the sending of his Son? Why, therefore, until the fullness of time, did he keep suppressing the treasure of his salvation? It is necessary, then, that you laugh heartily at what Paul taught concerning the mystery being revealed in the proclamation of the gospel that was earlier hidden in God.[55] But now that the sound of the gospel is proclaimed, the righteousness of Christ reaches no one unless it is embraced by faith.

Where do you think this faith comes from? If you reply, "from hearing," this is indeed true, but it comes not without the special revelation of the Spirit. Isaiah exclaims with amazement how few receive the revelation of God's arm (Isa. 53:1). Paul uses this passage as a testimony when he restricts the gift of faith to the elect (Rom. 10:16), but you do not allow any distinction. Christ indeed cries out, "Come to me all who labor" (Matt. 11:28), but also he cries out in another place, "No one can come to me unless the Father who sent me draws him" (John 6:44). Nor does he fight his own tail when inviting all to himself without exception by the external voice of the gospel. Yet he says that no one perceives anything unless it is given to him from heaven and that no one comes to him unless they are given to him by the Father (John 6:44).

There is another passage that you also shamelessly pollute with your snout, by declaring that all men who come into this world are illumined with the light of Christ's righteousness (John 1:9). As if John does not immediately afterwards add, "The light shines in the darkness and the darkness has not overcome it" (1:5). With these words he signifies that whatever reason and intelligence was given to man from the beginning has been suffocated and nearly destroyed. No other remedy remains except that Christ illuminates the blind. It is indeed true that Christ denied no one mercy who asked for it, but you do not recognize that such vows and prayers are being expressed by the Holy Spirit. Indeed faith, which is the fruit of free election, is the key that opens the entrance to prayer.

---

[55]Eph. 3:9–10.

So long as you are ignorant of these basic principles, the gospel is no different from the mysteries of Proserpine and Bacchus, and you even exalt the latter.[56] It is a wonder that any among the Christians could be found entangling themselves with such extraordinary errors.

In so far as you say that my disciples have been fashioned to be like my God, being crude, envious, calumnious, proud, carrying one thing in their tongue and another in their heart, I will set out to refute your ridiculous accusations not so much by words but by facts. Since I have no delight in slander, let your shameful acts remain unnoticed by me, except to say that it is lawful and worth the effort for me, in the presence of God, to testify briefly this one thing. When I fed you in my home,[57] no man had ever appeared to be more proud or more deceitful or more destitute than you. Whoever does not perceive you to be an imposter and a cynic devoted to shamelessness, and a buffoon barking against piety, they are absolutely without judgment.

I want to know for what you accuse me of cruelty, unless you perhaps refer to the death of your master Servetus.[58] But enough concerning me; this is more than sufficient. What kind of fruits my doctrine produces not only in this city but far and wide through many lands, I leave for the readers' investigation. From this school, which you so atrociously castigate, God himself daily chooses victims of the most noble and sweetest odor for the purpose of giving glory to the doctrine of his gospel. The students there, the number of whom is at least not displeasing, follow a meager and difficult manner of

---

[56]Both Prosperine, daughter of Zeus and Demeter, and Bacchus, son of Zeus and Semele, figure in ancient mystery religion.
[57]This is evidently a reference to the time that Castellio lodged in Calvin's home in Strasbourg.
[58]After Servetus had been condemned to burn by the Genevan authorities, Calvin without success interceded with them to have the mode of execution changed.

life, but yet they endure this life with supreme patience and gentleness. Desiring to be free from their former luxury, they willingly and peacefully adorn themselves with frugality. By denying themselves and this world, they all aspire to the hope of blessed immortality.

But since it is not expedient for me to boast, let the Lord of grace answer for me by stretching forth his favor upon his doctrine for the purpose of defending that same doctrine, which is in vain slandered by your foul insults. I sincerely desire to know from you: at the time you began to favor this doctrine, what was your condition? You reckon that it was not satisfactorily understood by you, because you were kept constricted by my authority. Because of this, you thought that it was unlawful to judge otherwise. But it must certainly be that you were too dull, because you were not able to understand what I have taught you, both in the familiarity of my own home and also what you heard when I so often preached in the public assembly. Now there are many qualified to bear witness that although I in vainly attempted in all sorts of ways to correct and heal your depraved nature, you still greatly professed to be one of my followers. You were being restrained by a bridle so that your unbridled licentiousness with which you sought to exalt the impiety that you now glorify may be seen as the cause of your deserved alienation.

You say that you pay attention not to who is speaking but to what is said. If only you might previously have been persuaded by this in order to be genuinely affected by the labor of others, so that you might have been skillfully trained. Now, since your only strengths are audacity and loquacity, you procure kindness by treating others with contempt. For my part, I claim nothing for myself; but I consider this to be deserved from the church, that if I am attributed a place among the faithful servants of God, then my authority should not be despised. If you said that a few unlearned men depended upon my nod or were moved by my fame, you might have provided some concrete evidence to defend your calumny.

Now, while you make out that it is my fault that illiterate men are not pleased with my doctrine, who will believe you that learned and ingenious men alone make sense of my books? Even more, who will believe that men are kept by authority alone from making a judgment? Therefore, we will prove that by your authority nothing is plausible except that which is accepted by the vulgar. This is certainly the reason why you deter everyone from gaining liberal learning, and you boast among your followers that study is empty and frivolous (the same study that is employed in philosophy, logic, and even theology) in order that you might gain more disciples for yourself. You deny that those who followed Christ were of this kind, as if the Christian faith was contrary to sound learning.

Here let the readers pay close attention to what the difference is between you and me. I declare that the wisest of men, until they become fools and pray to put away their own understanding and to assign themselves to meek simplicity in service to Christ, remain blinded by their pride and never taste the heavenly doctrine. For human reason is completely unable to taste the mysteries of God, and by itself human acuteness is dull. Therefore, I declare that humility is the beginning of true wisdom, which removes carnal understanding from us all, so that faith may acquire reverence for the mysteries of God. You, on the other hand, request that untutored men who despise all learning and are inflated only with the breath of arrogance appear in public so that they may audaciously make judgments concerning the mysteries of heaven. You do not acknowledge anyone as a legitimate judge except those who, being content with vulgar understanding, boldly reject what is not pleasing to them.

Paul will easily answer another of your insults with which you abuse my disciples, who, upon his authority, are inclined to abandon you and the heretics like you rather than to have their ears polluted by hearing your blasphemies. You deny this to be the proper principle on which to act because you believe that all should be entitled to a hearing, as if he said in vain, "As for a person who stirs up division, after warning him once and then twice, have nothing more to do with him" (Titus 3:10). If anyone refused to hear you, you would have a reason to complain. But you were permitted freedom to blabber, even being summoned and dragged to the public assembly, until you were removed from residing with us. Where is the limit if pious ears must always be open until they are satiated with your slander of God? When you are ridiculing all pious principles, then you are more than pleased. Do you wish to believe that the sons of God were so stupid that they would either smile upon your licentiousness or not be moved by your sacrilegious insults?

Concerning the issue itself, I am confident that I have answered you so that all readers of sound mind might easily observe that the Spirit, who gives a mouth and wisdom, has not been withheld from me. If you proceed to resist the Spirit, you will produce a stubbornness that will be equal only with your disgrace. I will not cease to desire and pray, though I barely have courage to hope, that you might finally yield to the revealed truth. Concerning the final cavil you throw out, that I am not to be angry at your insults if I believe your writing was necessary—for me this is truly a serious and efficacious exhortation to endurance, because nothing is more useful or apt for restraining indignation than the admonition of David: "If he is cursing because the LORD has said to him, 'Curse David,' who then shall say, 'Why have you done so?'" (2 Sam. 16:10). David knew that Shimei was inspired to utter insults by the same madness by which you now are aroused. But he reckoned that the same attacks that Shimei made at random were being governed by the secret providence of God, so for this reason David restrained himself. No man will ever bear the insults of the Devil and the wicked with calm moderation unless he turns his thoughts from them and toward God alone. May God restrain you, Satan. AMEN

Geneva, 9th January, 1558.

SCRIPTURE INDEX